"Denise will be known for her pioneering work in building a preschool that not only perfected the power of play but turned in the requisite achievements in both her gifted and special charges.

With detail and intensity, this book takes the reader through the preschool "wilderness" of the late 1990s to 2000s and the hit-and-miss changes by the government in this sector. It would really be fitting for parents, teachers, administrators, and policymakers to take heed—to regroup and recall that teaching is really about the heart and soul."

— **Hwee Goh**
Wee Care Mother of four, 2005-13; TV Journalist, Media Consultant, and Author

"Whether you are an educator, parent, entrepreneur, policymaker, Singaporean or otherwise, you will find Denise's autoethnography to be a gloriously beautiful yet painfully familiar—or perhaps cathartic—read. You may not agree with her convictions or decisions, but you will no doubt be challenged and inspired by her unparalleled intelligence, vulnerable eloquence, visionary leadership, and above all, her deep and abiding faith and passion."

— **Dr Lydia L. S. Chan**
Member, Board of Governors and Chairperson, Council, Yew Chung College of Early Childhood Education

"More than just the trials and tribulations of starting a business, *Preschool in the Wilderness* offers a warm, sincere, and insightful take on Denise's journey on setting up and finally letting go of Wee Care. She takes us in depth into the realm of special needs education and preschool education, as she navigates and charts her own path whilst wearing different hats, sharing her joys, challenges, and frustrations. An intriguing and provocative read for all parents."
    — **Isabella Loke**
       Wee Care Mother, 2011-14

"Denise tells the story of her 21-year journey in what she calls the early childhood wilderness in Singapore. She tells of her experiences in the multiple roles she played ... as a teacher, business owner, leader, curriculum designer, mother. She shares the joys and struggles, relationships and conflicts, insights and tensions in her daily life as an early childhood educator and as the wilderness is slowly transformed by the changes taking place over time. Whether we read to listen to the voice of an early childhood educator in Singapore, or to ponder on the changes and issues that are part of our nation's journey in early childhood, there is something to prompt us to reflect on who we are in this early childhood community and our place in this wilderness."
    — **Dr Hanin Hussain**
       Senior Lecturer/Assistant Head (Early Childhood), Psychology and Child & Human Development Academic Group, National Institute of Education-Nanyang Technological University

"It has been quite a while since I have read a book till the early hours of the morning. As I was drawn deeper and deeper into the author's journey, I had to complete it. Throughout the book, her account of the dilemma between her idealism and realism, struggles between what is good for each child and the balance sheet, fulfilling regulatory requirements and a host of other professional predicaments, is personal yet objective. Her decisions are ably supported by citations of facts and well-conducted research findings. She has rightly described her narration as an autoethnography.

Though this book is written with parents, academicians, and policymakers in mind, many operators and principals, especially those who value quality early childhood education, will be able to identify with Denise. All early childhood educators, whether they are principals or practitioners, as well as parents, will benefit from this book as it provides so many insights into the operation of early childhood organisations, which include parents' aspirations and demands, staff well-being, and regulatory requirements. It should be on the recommended reading list for early childhood trainees. The only let-down is the end of the journey; while I understand Denise's reason for walking away after spending more than 20 years of her life to build the renowned Wee Care in Singapore, I would have preferred a happier ending."

— **Datuk Dr Chiam Heng Keng**
Founding President, Early Childhood Care & Education Council, Malaysia

"This book is a must-read for at least three groups of people: devoted professionals, policymakers, and parents of young children. It demonstrates the workability of a business model for running a "new" kind of preschool. Denise documents her innovative and enduring endeavours, with strong personal reflections, to operate Wee Care in a way that was financially self-sustainable, creative, honest, and most of all, committed to prioritising children's and parents' needs. When developing public policies, policymakers should be able to learn from this book to remove unnecessary hindrances and facilitate devoted professionals to deliver high-quality services. Parents can also reflect on what it means to choose the "right" kind of nursery or kindergarten for their child."

— **Professor Ly-Yun Chang**
Institute of Sociology, Academia Sinica, Taiwan

"I am privileged to count Dr Denise Lai as one of my old friends from Junior College. Like her, I started out at a Methodist kindergarten because it was walking distance from my three-room flat. And reading this memoir of Denise's years running Wee Care, I almost feel glad that she did not read "A" Level Economics, as I did, since that may have held her back from her labour of love to establish an innovative company that made an important contribution to Singapore's preschool landscape. Denise's memoirs document the challenges that many entrepreneurs face: dealing with high rents, intense competition, sometimes unreasonable customer expectations, challenges with hiring and retaining good team members; and having to navigate regulations that often seem as onerous as they are insufficiently catered to ground realities. But Denise also describes—in down-to-earth, crisp prose—how passion and idealistic conviction can make all the difference in one's journey as a preschool educator and also as an entrepreneur. That passion was lovingly woven into Wee Care's practices, processes, and ethos; and can be found on every page of this book. Denise's memoirs are also a cautionary tale for policymakers, about the need to cultivate diversity, innovation, and experimentation in our educational landscape, so as to nurture in our citizens the confidence, initiative, and character that today's world—and, dare I say it, economy—demands."

— **Leon Perera**
Member of Parliament, Aljunied GRC Singapore

"An honest and heartfelt account of a trailblazing journey in the "preschool wilderness", replete with all the bumps, bruises, and triumphs along the way. A wonderful reminder that as parents, we want our children to be taught and led by educators who, above all else, have a heart to serve and a desire to care for them. A unique and multifaceted book that will resonate not only with parents and educators, but also with working mothers, entrepreneurs, and anyone who is on a life journey led by a calling."

— **L. K. Tong**
Wee Care Mother, 2011-17

"This book offers a captivating first-person account of an early childhood professional, giving voice to a teacher, one whose role is critical in the life of almost every person, yet whose voice is not given the hearing it deserves (and needs). It is also the voice of a woman, a mother, a female leader, and employer—with each role adding another layer to create a rich, nuanced, eventful, and reflective representation of the multiple dimensions that add up to a preschool.

The value of the narrative lies in that it not only presents the author's intense and varied experience but it also embeds and highlights the underlying theoretical framework, pedagogical practices, significance of play, and relationships with children and parents that informed her work.

This book comes as a warm and timely guide—as well as a cautionary tale—to those involved in the emerging pre-school system in any country."

    — **Dr Priti Joshi**
    Associate Professor, Department of Human
    Development & Childhood Studies, Lady Irwin College,
    University of Delhi, India

PRESCHOOL IN THE WILDERNESS

Traversing Joy, Grief, and Hope in
Singapore's Early Childhood Landscape

Denise Lai Chua
Ed.D. (Dual Award)

Candid Creation Publishing

First published 2021

Copyright © 2021 Denise Lai Chua

All rights reserved. No part of this publication may be reproduced, stored in a retrieval system, or transmitted, in any form or by any means, electronic, mechanical, photocopying, recording or otherwise, without the prior permission of the publisher, except for inclusion of brief quotations in a review.

Candid Creation Publishing books are available through most major bookstores in Singapore. For bulk order of our books at special quantity discounts, please email us at enquiry@candidcreation.com.

PRESCHOOL IN THE WILDERNESS
Traversing Joy, Grief, and Hope in Singapore's Early Childhood Landscape

Author : Denise Lai Chua
Publisher : Phoon Kok Hwa
Editor : Patricia Ng
Cover designer : Ryanne Ng
Layout : Corrine Teng
Published by : Candid Creation Publishing LLP
167 Jalan Bukit Merah
#05-12 Connection One Tower 4
Singapore 150167
Website : www.candidcreation.com
Facebook : www.facebook.com/CandidCreationPublishing
Email : enquiry@candidcreation.com

National Library Board, Singapore Cataloguing in Publication Data

Name(s): Lai Chua, Denise.
Title: Preschool in the wilderness : traversing joy, grief and hope in Singapore's early childhood landscape / Denise Lai Chua.
Description: Singapore : Candid Creation Publishing, 2021.
Identifier(s): ISBN 978-981-17078-7-2 (paperback)
Subject(s): LCSH: Lai Chua, Denise. | Early childhood educators--Singapore--Biography. | Early childhood education--Singapore.
Classification: DDC 372.21092--dc23

CONTENTS

Introduction xi

1   Mapping the Terrain 1
2   Building a Shelter 18
3   Cultivating Curriculum 31
4   Welcoming New Life 45
5   Caring, Mothering, Loving, Teaching 57
6   Playing All the Time 70
7   Surviving the Competition 84
8   Navigating Blame and Responsibility 97
9   Braving Drought and Famine 111
10   Planting More 124
11   Sharing Fruit 140
12   Growing Up, Growing Old 155
13   Walking Away 168

Epilogue 189

INTRODUCTION

To my knowledge, there has not been a first-person account yet written about the interiority of early childhood teaching in Singapore. Not a sensational "tell-all" or mundane descriptions of classroom activities and how these relate to meeting learning goals, mind you. Rather, a sincere portrayal of what it is like to work with young children in this country, one that is as honest as possible, however subjective and biased.

I think there are many reasons for this gap. Other than the very understandable limitations of time and inclination (preschool teachers, like other helping and service professionals, have probably been on their feet all day), there are doubts too, I believe, about the perceived value of preschool teachers' stories. Indeed, over the course of writing this book, I wondered (and worried) many times whether it would be bought, appreciated, and/or read. Would anyone be interested, or care? Why should or would they care?

The doubts themselves are probably caused by a multitude of factors, all impinging on what educationalists have termed, the teacher's "voice". But surely, you must be thinking, how ironic! A teacher speaks all day and is often heard. My own memories here are vivid: All through primary school, the teachers—whose lessons I had to endure—always seemed to be shouting.

But "voice" in this context is something else altogether. When used in research, it refers to "voice" in the metaphorical sense, as a way of knowing. And so, on the basis of this definition, what I really mean are "different voices, voices traditionally silenced or marginalised". The aim in acknowledging these voices is to empower them; and … as it relates to teaching specifically, "to recognise the message of a voice steeped in the relational world of children—the voice of those who cannot (and should not) separate themselves from that world in an effort to understand it".[1]

Finding and listening to the teacher's voice, however, is not always easy; some have claimed it has "been long silenced". I know that I have been in situations where I have wanted to hear preschool teachers say more, say "no" (and this, not to children), or simply say something sooner. Unfortunately, I also know that the act of "voice" for early childhood carers and educators in Singapore is fraught with many pitfalls. I attribute this to the distinctive cultural (and with this, I also mean the economic and political) milieu that we inhabit. As I recount in this book, I myself have been silenced by the play of power in my homeland, by the pressures of trying to make a living in a capitalist society, and by the notions of what I "should" do or be as a woman, mother, teacher, female leader, and employer. At times, these latter forms of shushing have come from other women themselves. While I have understood the reasons why, it has not made the task of emboldening self and others, in the name of social justice, easier.

At the same time, I also know that the personal reprieves I have had in being able to speak up and speak out **in spite of** my womanhood are probably a direct result of the education I have been privileged to receive. But even here, there have been the costs presented by an education and social system so stratified that I have sometimes been written off very quickly as an "Other" by other early childhood professionals (and perhaps even other academics or policymakers) without a deeper consideration of who I really am or what I am saying about a plausible vision for early childhood care and education in Singapore.

> She's too
> high,
> low,
> broad,
> narrow …
> vested,
> emotional,
> careless,
> forthright,
> unwise,
> impracticable.

I hope that this book will succeed in addressing some of that distance (at the risk of inadvertently reinforcing the negative views) so that my voice may be counted as one amongst many in an environment that has not traditionally favoured more vocal forms of representation.

Again, I want to reiterate that "voice" here does not revolve around the mere asking of questions or the deferential act of making suggestions. I prefer to think of it as the act of being "intelligently disruptive without destroying anything"² —anything other than the myths or beliefs that constrain and limit us, of course. As I illustrate in future chapters, we need to have a stronger and more coherent voice about the power we want neoliberalism* and politics to have over ourselves as early childhood carers, educators, and providers,** as well as the children and families of Singapore.

In this way then, I hope that this book will achieve two goals for the reader who may be an early childhood professional. First, I hope that it will express stories that will be familiar to you, to communicate the reality of having "been there and done that: the feeds, the pees, and the poos"—and in so doing, to say most of all, that you are seen, you are heard, you are understood, and you are appreciated.

At the same time, I hope that within the analyses and discussions embedded in the stories will be perspectives that will encourage you to think further and critically, and forthwith to question why things are the way they are. I say this because children cannot be educated effectively without you. You matter. Your thoughts and feelings matter. Your aspirations and experiences matter.

As I trawl the memories of the stories of my past, please consider your present and imagine what a better future for you and your students should look like; and more importantly, to do this

---

* One of the main tenets in neoliberalism is that human flourishing requires an economic context where capitalists are facilitated to maximise their profits.

** From here on, I will use the phrase, "early childhood professional" to refer to all who spend most of their working hours in a care or educational setting with and for young children. However, there will also be times when "early childhood educators" or "preschool teachers" might be used interchangeably. Further, as the boundaries between caring and teaching are less obvious these days, I will not make a distinction between childcare and preschool teachers (as all are "teachers") unless it is for a specific point I am seeking to make.

without fear, even when it seems excessively demonstrative and/ or "un-Singaporean". We tend to denigrate the importance of feelings in Singapore, relegating this always to the back burner in favour of hard, objective data. But even Science makes assumptions about what is true. We can acknowledge our subjectivities and say that our ways of knowing are important too. Our very passion for teaching, our love for children, cannot be detached from who we are, what we think and feel, and what we want to say. Indeed, may this give you the courage to speak so that your voice can and will be heard. And if you are a preschool teacher outside of Singapore, I hope that you will find important similarities and differences in the stories and topics covered; patterns and principles that will help inform **your** practice and guide you in finding **your** voice in **your** context.

I should add at this point that this book has also been written with three other audiences in mind: parents, academics, and policymakers, but each for different reasons. When I was researching material for the last chapter, "Walking Away", I was painfully reminded that one of the findings from the Reach government survey about the proposed (at the time) Early Childhood Development Centres Regulatory Framework was some parents saying that "fines and financial penalties may not be an effective deterrent against larger operators ... [the parents] suggested more punitive measures, such as a prison term".[3]

Now, I am not a fan of large conglomerates (for reasons that I hope will become obvious in this book). I am also acutely conscious, over the years, that some children have received poor care in some preschools. Yet, the harsh feedback made me wonder, truly, what some parents perceive of the working life of early childhood professionals; whether they understand how challenging it is without the further and constant threat of punishment hanging over the teachers' heads.

While this book may not succeed in shifting a parent's dissatisfaction significantly, I hope it will provide, at the very least, a perspective that unearths the deep and essential humanity in preschool teachers, and how supporting and encouraging them will do more for one's child than threats or punishment ever will.

Having said this, we also know that not all parents are harsh. In fact, the vast majority of parents who came through Wee Care's doors over my 21 years at the school were kind, patient, and loving. I learnt as much from them as their children did from me and my teachers. To each one of you: Thank you so much for the years of unceasing and unstinting support. I owe you a debt of gratitude for the friendship you have shown and continue to show me. I hope that this book will not be inscrutable; that it will remind you of the wonderful times your children had at Wee Care, and that it will also clarify moments, perhaps, when my decisions seemed a little strange or incomprehensible. Indeed, for those of you who had to bear the terrible inconveniences that arose after my departure, thank you. Thank you for remaining with the new management and with the teachers. Thank you for showing the grace that you did.

Given the subject matter of this book, one or two academics might be willing, perhaps, to give it a read. I should pre-empt their/your expectations by saying that this volume is quite unfortunately, not an academic treatise. I had the option of spending the past year getting my work into a peer-reviewed journal or writing this book. I chose the latter; mainly because I wanted the material to be as available and accessible as possible, and also because I felt it had to be written as a somewhat countervailing **personal voice** to the dominant discourses circulating about the quality, affordability, and accessibility of early childhood education in Singapore currently. For instance, there have been papers written about the evils of private preschools and the rabid commercialism that pervades this sector.[4] There have also been many strong-arm policy tactics levied, in tandem with clever economic strategies, to trim the sector down to a manageable size and form.

Absent from these discussions, quite sadly, has been the experiences of small- and medium-sized kindergartens and their owners, many of whom were in the notable position of providing for the education of Singapore's young when there was no or little government support to speak of. This book is my attempt at a more nuanced assessment, cradled within a gentle Foucauldian-like unarchiving of the genealogy of preschool education in Singapore. Written notwithstanding from the perspective of one woman and one institution, this account will admittedly be limited and limiting. Yet, I hope it will be useful data to the educational thinkers, researchers, and trainers who continue to observe, comment, and influence what early childhood education should be and look like in our wonderful nation. In particular, the following chapters might provide helpful local material for thought and discussion in teacher-training and ongoing professional development sessions:

- What sort of curriculum really matters in early childhood education? (Chapter 3)
- What forms of relationship should we be seeking to develop with parents and families? (Chapters 4 and 8)
- Is it good, right, and appropriate for early childhood educators to love their students? (Chapter 5)
- Can our children truly play? (Chapters 6 and 7)
- Can old teachers teach young children? (Chapter 12)
- Who, ultimately, is responsible for early childhood education in Singapore? (Chapter 13 and Epilogue)

At the same time, academic thinkers may be interested to know that in order to accommodate my desire to blend both experiences and analysis into a narrative form, the style that this book is written in may best be described as an autoethnography. This term, "autoethnography", comprises three different words: "auto", "ethno-", and "graphy," which together signify the textual rendering of one's personal experiences within the researcher's social, political, economic, and cultural context.[5] Autoethnography has elsewhere been depicted as "ethnographic in its methodological orientation, cultural in its interpretive orientation and autobiographical in its content orientation".[6] Explained yet another way, a memoir would have written the personal story without any theory. An autoethnography is a memoir refracted through the prism of a researching, enquiring, and conceptualising mind.[7]

There are different kinds of autoethnographies. The one that found more resonance within my soul—and this again, of woman, mother, teacher, female leader—may aptly be described as the evocative form.[8] This style demands a type of writing that is vulnerable, empathic[9] and heartfelt.[10] It assumes a struggle to make meaning within particular contexts.

Applied thus, the acts of remembering that I undertook for each chapter/topic were intertwined, sometimes painfully, with reflexive acts of self-examination: my beliefs, judgements, and practices. Inevitably, I had to come to terms with baring my soul: the good, the bad and the ugly, the emotions and attitudes, my spirituality and non-spirituality, my biases and self-justifications. It would have been easier, without a doubt, to have walked away from this; or hidden my aims behind a survey or interview questions of others, all shrouded by the good practice of objectivity, distance, and participant confidentiality."** Yet, I hope the honesty of this book will be taken for what it is, an attempt ultimately to open up more conversations about what we want, collectively and inclusively, for early childhood education in Singapore. Wherever any portion reads like narcissism or self-absorption, I ask for your kind forbearance. All flaws, errors, or omissions are mine. I am also obliged to warn you of the high chance of banality—the occasional expressions of poetic verse may not be of literary merit. Nonetheless, I trust that this book will be a valuable read, and that it will not fail to bring insights and a different perspective to the table.

Last but not least, for the politician or policymaker who may indulge this narrative with some of his/her time and consideration, I only ask that you understand how betrayed some of us felt following the sweeping measures that were implemented after 2012 in the name of "quality" and good practice. While teachers have never, historically, "been an important source of information for educational change,"[11] they are, nonetheless, the very ones you need to effect such change. More importantly, there is an "ineluctable connection between their well-being and the well-being of children".[12] I hope that this book will encourage you to reconcile the "hard truths"[13] with the "hard choices"[14] that were presented to you; yet steer you to assess the human costs of what was decided. It is still not too late to forge a better way.

*** Pseudonyms have been used throughout this book, except for the names of colleagues and associates who have granted permission to be identified.

1. Llorens, M. B. (1994). Action research: Are teachers finding their voice? *The Elementary School Journal, 95*(1), 3–10.
2. Brown, L. M., & Gilligan, C. (1992). *Meeting at the crossroads.* New York: Ballantine.
3. Early Childhood Development Agency (2015). *Public consultation on proposed Early Childhood Development Centres Regulatory Framework: Summary of key feedback and responses.* REACH (Reaching Everyone for Active Citizenry @ Home). https://www.reach.gov.sg/participate/public-consultation/early-childhood-development-agency/public-consultation-on-proposed-early-childhood-development-centres-regulatory-framework
4. Lim, S. (2017). Marketisation and corporatisation of early childhood care and education in Singapore. In M. Li, J. Fox, & S. Grieshaber (Eds.), *Contemporary issues and challenge in early childhood education in the Asia-Pacific region* (pp.17–32). Singapore: Springer.
5. Luitel, B., & Taylor, P. (2003, Aug. 9). *Critiquing situatedness: An integrated approach to improve a researcher's practice.* [Paper presentation] Annual Forum of the Western Australian Institute for Educational Research (WAIER). Edith Cowan University, Mount Lawley, WA, Australia.
6. Chang, H. (2008). *Autoethnography as method.* Walnut Creek, CA: Left Coast Press.
7. Scott, J. D. (2014). Memoir as a form of auto-ethnographic research for exploring the practice of transnational higher education in China. *Higher Education Research & Development, 33*(4), 757–768.
8. Ellis, C. S., & Bochner, A. P. (2006). Analyzing analytic autoethnography: An autopsy. *Journal of Contemporary Ethnography, 35*(4), 429–449.
9. Muncey, T. (2010). *Creating autoethnographies.* London, UK: Sage.
10. Ellis, C. (1999). Heartful autoethnography, *Qualitative Health Research, 9*(5), 669–683.
11. Llorens, M. B. (1994). Action research: Are teachers finding their voice? *The Elementary School Journal, 95*(1), 3–10.
12. Bullough Jr., R. V. (2008). The writing of teachers' lives: Where personal troubles and social issues meet. *Teacher Education Quarterly, 35*(4), 7–26.
13. Han, F. K., Ibrahim, Z., Chua, M. H., Lim, L., Low, I., Lin, R., Chan, R. (2011). *Lee Kuan Yew: Hard truths to keep Singapore going.* Singapore: Straits Times Press.
14. Low, D., & Vadaketh, S. T. (2014). *Hard choices: Challenging the Singapore consensus.* Singapore: NUS Press.

1

MAPPING THE TERRAIN

I would not call motherhood a wilderness. No, motherhood is a garden, a beautiful garden where I am constantly seeding, watering, pruning, shaping, admiring, loving; always loving, even when there are weeds that need pulling and bugs that need spraying.

Go away! Scat, you do not belong here!

It is a special place. But I know it is special only to me. Other mothers have their own gardens and every garden is different. Fathers, too, work in their gardens differently. They see and plan and care for their gardens differently from mothers. That is what I think anyway.

You can say that I love my garden but really, I love all we have managed to grow in it. I always will.

One tree in my garden is 25 years old now. She is strong, strong in all the right ways ... I think and hope and pray. Strong in her arms, strong in her unrelenting views of the world from her height. I take another look, as I have many times before. She is not the tallest tree—she never will be— but she is the oldest tree in my garden, and she is strong, strong, strong.

May you be strong but flexible, unyielding but also yielding. May your roots go deep, deep, deep and cling to the Rock inside.

The irony is, it was this tree that made me venture out into the wilderness.

She was just a sapling when we returned to Singapore. I tried, tried my best to work outside of our plot. But I would keep thinking about her throughout the workday and wonder.

Are you thriving with Grandpa and Grandma? Are you missing me? Did Rosie remember it was eight ounces, not six?

The wilderness seemed like a big place. I should have been daunted. But I was not.

I only saw the possibilities of what some of that space could be for my saplings and other saplings; imagined the creation of oases with connections of relationships and resources criss-crossing between life-giving wells of creative ideas and hope, of friendships and joy, of music and art and conversation and play.

It was a wilderness, but I stepped into it to find—and to bring from it—life.

I spent my preschool years in Singapore in the 1970s in two kindergartens. The first was ensconced in a Methodist church, within easy walking distance of my parents' three-room HDB* flat. I must have been five. The only thing I remember of that year was eating White Rabbit candy and old-fashioned melt-in-your-mouth "snow white cakes" for the first time. I also remember what the photographs

---

* HDB, or the Housing and Development Board, is responsible for all public housing in Singapore. It is a statutory board under the Ministry of National Development.

tell me, that my mother came with a cake to celebrate my birthday with the rest of the class. I wore my best dress for the celebration, something of a thick velvet-like pinafore which I would not have wanted to wear at other times. Singapore is far too hot for extra layers.

The next year, my parents carted me off to another kindergarten. It was run by the Catholic church and I cried and cried the first few days I was there. One day, my Malay nanny, Hawal, said to me, "Denise, don't cry. Look through the windows there. I will wait for you at the back of the building. You will be able to see my umbrella." I believed her, stopped crying, and kept looking up at the vent windows that whole morning. It was not till many years later that I realised Hawal had told a little white lie to stop me crying.

I have other memories from that year in kindergarten. For instance, I remember being made to memorise the times table and being challenged to recall and write the answers out as fast as possible. I remember that we had opportunities for water play too. But the play was always rationed. We had to take turns and there were never enough pots and funnels to go around. Worse, the time spent pouring and splashing was always far too short for my liking.

My brother, who was one year younger than me, was in the classroom next to mine. His teacher was a tall Chinese lady called Mrs Tan. There was a wall separating our classrooms, but at one end of the wall, near the teacher's table, was a break with a small gate. We would stand on our side of the gate and talk to our younger peers in the other room. The teachers could communicate with one another too; or move freely across both classrooms whenever they had something to do.

One day, I noticed my brother crying at the gate. I ran to see what was wrong. He had gone back to his seat and there were children crowding around him. I panicked and tried to get someone's attention. What was wrong? Mrs Tan was sitting stone-faced at her desk and ignoring me.

I plucked up my courage, asked my teacher for permission to leave the classroom, then headed straight to my brother's classroom where I asked Mrs Tan if I could speak with him. She gave a small, sharp nod and I sprinted over.

What's wrong? Why are you crying?

He did not answer me. But his friends were able to fill me in. Apparently, he had been playing with his handkerchief in class, using it like a catapult, and Mrs Tan had confiscated it as punishment.

I took out my handkerchief and pushed it into his hands.

Here, here, you can have mine. Stop crying.

I have no idea if Mrs Tan ever returned my brother's handkerchief, but for me, it was just another day shouldering part of my world as Big Sister.

It is amazing how much children can remember. Studies have shown that new and interesting experiences can wield powerful effects in the formation of intact autobiographic memories. In particular, the most powerful memories are not just what the child saw or did but the emotional content of the experience, content that is oftentimes, uniquely personal to the child.[15]

> What do you remember, Baby?
> My paintings hanging
> on the black window grilles

in the dining area and
the playground downstairs,
being forced to eat fish porridge while
our neighbour's fierce dog barked and
the *makcik*^{**} selling frozen popsicles on
the walk from our flat to the MRT Station
went past a school.

Importantly, research studies have also shown that a child's ability to recall events improves when parents talk about the past in a rich and elaborate manner.[16] In fact, this echoes the generally accepted fact that the number of words a child is exposed to before the age of four is significantly correlated with future outcomes in the child's life. In other words, one of the most important things parents can do for their children is to talk to—and with—them consistently.[17]

It was this desire to do what was right for Baby 1 that started me exploring. She was crawling and toddling about at this time. I remember singing, rocking, talking, playing, and reading stories to her, and yet thinking, feeling, pining...

This is not enough. This cannot be enough. I am not enough. She needs friends. She needs more.

I began calling the kindergartens and childcare centres that were listed in the Yellow Pages. These business directories were large heavy tomes that sat underneath our "modern" cordless telephone in the living room.

I am sorry, Mrs Lai, your child is too young. Register her for the pre-nursery programme in our kindergarten when she is three years old.

**   *Makcik* is a Malay word, a polite term of address for a middle-aged or elderly Malay woman who may or may not be a relative.

No, no, Mrs Lai. We cannot accept children who are 15 months old. The Ministry of Community Development stipulates that children must be 18 months old at least.

"But I will stay with her," I sputtered. "You will not have to do anything. I just want her to be with other children, just to watch them running around, playing, talking ... please. I will pay the fees but visit for only an hour or two a day ... please."

It was, to be honest, like talking to the desert wind. All I felt I got back each time I opened my mouth was a mouthful of sand.

Where on earth had they pulled these magic numbers from? Babies start learning the minute they are born. They are learning through their senses, they are learning the language we speak, they are learning about themselves, about us, about the world. Oh my poor, lonely baby.

It felt personal ... and frustrating. The range of preschool provisions in Singapore in the 1990s was like a veritable wilderness. Little did I fully understand then that the reasons for this dearth were historical, political, and economic.

Historical because as a new nation, Singapore had had far more problems to tackle than preschool education at the time of its independence. Political and economic because according to the People's Action Party (PAP) government (the party that has ruled Singapore for more than 60 years), Singapore (always) has to be prudent with its financial resources. The country simply cannot afford to pursue a welfare orientation in public policies. There are many more pressing concerns to focus on, including food and water security, national defence, healthcare, housing, and so on.

Hence, although preschool provisions had been established in Singapore in the 1960s, there was no systematic training of teachers until 1969. The Teachers' Training College took responsibility for training from 1977 and this continued until the college became the Institute of Education in 1981. Training for childcare teachers began in 1985 only. During this period, there were about 50 childcare centres for the whole of Singapore, with a little more than 100 staff employed.[18] In direct contrast, approximately 40,000 babies were being born each year![19]

At the same time, as early as the 1960s, the Government tended to view secondary education as being the more profitable investment.[20] They had calculated the rate of return to society after completing secondary education to be 18.2% for males and 17.0% for females. What is more, in 1968, the Ministry of Finance had concluded that Singapore lacked a sufficient number of technically trained workers to meet the requirements of new industries. An emphasis was subsequently given to technical education. The Vocational Industrial Training Board (VITB) was birthed from this assessment, the predecessor of the current Institute of Technical Education (ITE).[21]

When early childhood settings were established, they were construed as acts of charity and regarded as a functional first step towards formal education. PAP kindergartens in the 1960s were conducted in any space available—from wayang (street opera) stages to shophouses. That I was educated in church kindergartens in the 1970s was already a sign of progress!

It is probably true that children were being looked after by their own mothers, or extended family like grandparents and nannies (as I was) in the early years of Singapore's independence. But I do not think we can assert that there was no need, no demand, for professional early childhood services back then. The evidence persists to this day that Singaporean women generally find it hard to maintain a full-time career outside of their home because they have to shoulder important filial responsibilities in the home, especially in caring for the young and/or the elderly.[22] Women would like flexible working arrangements but these are not always available; when they do work, a gender pay gap is usually evident.

For me, it was certainly true that I stayed at home for a year for Baby 1 because I could not find adequate care and/or educational facilities outside. I did not want to burden my parents and at the same time, noticed that the quality of domestic help available for hire was not always reliable.

What do you want to watch on TV now, Baby? Shall we sing along?

Day after day, the hours fell into a predictable routine: walks in the morning and evening, visits to the children's community library for more and more books, sojourns to the shops for paint, crayons, paper, and pretend toys to *masak-masak****. We used the little plastic cutlery and utensils to feed all of her imaginary friends, from hard plastic dinosaurs to Ernie, Bert, and Elmo from Sesame Street. We painted bright faces and big trees on sheets of paper, decorated the concrete corridor outside our front door with shapes and splotches of water, then went to the playground for more play with sand and swings, slides, and see-saws.

How are other mothers coping? Are they worried like me? Are they bored like me? How can I ever go back to work again?

Progressively, in between the feeds and baths and naps, wandering somewhere across the community library and the floor of our kitchen, arising from whispered and half-spoken prayers, I imagined a space, a place, a programme perhaps, where babies could be taught and sung to; scenes where teachers played with infants and

---

***   *Masak* is the Malay word for cook. *Masak-masak* is a term used to describe playing with toys, particularly when children pretend to cook.

introduced them to all that was soft and sweet and sticky about our world, or rough and windy and grassy; interactions framed by words, mediated by touch, soothed by music and warmed with love, lots of love.

Aha! A network of visiting teachers. That is what we need.

I turned the concept around in my mind across multiple iterations, and gradually, Wee Care and the Baby Buddy Network took shape. For years after, many clients and business associates automatically assumed that my family name was "Wee". But the name "Wee Care" was, in fact, inspired by the orphanage that I had volunteered in during my husband's work-stint in Hong Kong in the mid-1990s. There, a unit called "Wee Care" had been formed exclusively for babies with special needs. It was a name both my husband and I loved because of the play on the word "wee" meaning small and "we", together.

More importantly, while set up as a business, Wee Care was genuinely pedagogical in both content and intention. It was a social enterprise in the days when the term "social enterprise" was not fully understood and certainly not a buzzword. But it was most definitely not a charity. I did not want Wee Care to be a charity. I wanted it to be able to sustain itself at the financial level. I wanted women to be able to carve out a livelihood around it, either as teachers or as clients who could leave for work knowing that a Baby Buddy would soon be arriving to play with and care for their infant. But most of all, I wanted it for Baby 1 and for others like her. Little did I know then that this decision to develop an educational business would eventually become my biggest and most heartfelt burden.

That I could register Wee Care as a business entity in 1997—very easily and in a highly straightforward manner—was a reflection of the liberal commercial environment that Singapore had established for itself since the mid-1960s. As the Baby Buddy Network involved home visits and the care and education of infants and toddlers, the nature of the work did not fall squarely into either of the neat categories of "kindergarten" or "childcare centre" that were regulated by the Ministry of Education (MOE) and the then Ministry of Community Development (MCD) respectively. In fact, as late as the 2010s, when Wee Care centres were already fully mature and operational facilities, there were still tensions and dilemmas in regulation: Our kindergartens came under the purview of the MOE but services for children with special needs came under the supervisory parameters of the Ministry of Social and Family Development (MSF) ... or actually, maybe it was the Committee for Private Education (CPE) ... or wait, no, maybe ....

See what I mean?

That education could be a "business" at all—a concept that has been deeply contested for decades internationally and more so in welfare economies—was much less of an issue in Singapore then, and perhaps so, even now. One need only consider the wide range of private tuition centres and enrichment schools that compete shoulder to shoulder for a piece of the local S$1.4 billion dollar tuition industry pie to know that there is a big "market";[23] a market, I would add, that has been aided in its growth by liberal (or should we say, prudent?) government economic policies.

In year 2000, Dr Aline Wong, then Senior Minister of State for Education, said:

> "MOE will not take over PSE (preschool education). The provision of PSE will remain firmly in the hands of the private and people sectors. There is merit in

allowing different centres with different philosophies and schools of thought to offer different types of PSE. It will also encourage creative innovation as each centre strives to meet the needs of its unique pupil profile."[24]

Ten years later, in a January 2010 parliamentary reply to a Member of Parliament who had asked whether pre-primary education would be made compulsory for all, then Minister of Education, Dr Ng Eng Hen, similarly stated that:

"... a nationalised preschool sector would tend towards conformity, which is not ideal. It would deprive parents the ability to choose from a variety of early childhood care and education models and operators that best fits the needs of their child."[25]

The government's attitude towards preschool education shifted abruptly in 2012. But in 1997, I was completely naïve and oblivious to these tensions. I was instead overjoyed that I was now a business owner, albeit one who cared very deeply about the education of young children.

Most of that first year was spent designing a logo and brochure, printing letterheads and placing flyers in paediatric and obstetric clinics plus running first-aid workshops for parents and domestic helpers, in addition to caring for Baby 1 all at the same time. It was humbling and hard work but I learnt a great deal about not being "shy", about being thick-skinned when necessary. Indeed, I will always be grateful to the medical doctors who heard me out in the early years of

Wee Care, who understood my heart and who told their patients and clients about us.

We hired our first Baby Buddy in 1998. Jennifer was an American who had spent time as a nanny to four young children prior to coming to Singapore. She was assigned to an infant whose mother had a busy career and who was deeply worried that her son was not getting enough stimulation at home in the care of her elderly parent. Jennifer saw baby Zak two or three times a week. She spent the sessions reading and singing to him, playing and taking him swimming.

You know, he can now balance when I sit him on my back while swimming.

Jenn was a very conscientious Buddy but more importantly, she was an empathic and responsive caregiver to baby Zak. In addition to integrity, this was an essential criterion I had already concluded all Wee Care Baby Buddies had to have. Research has consistently shown that nurturing and responsive adults are crucial to optimal development in early childhood. Strong and stable attachments enhance coping mechanisms later in life including emotion regulation and increased competence. There is a profound impact on the quality of interaction between a baby and the adult if the adult's responses contain affirmations rather than prohibitions.[26]

At the end of every Baby Buddy session, Jenn would send a report of what she had done with Zak. We compiled these reports at the close of every month into a developmental summary which we would send to his parents. We also used these reports to track his progress and learning, everything from learning to eat, to walking then running, and eventually talking. It was exciting and exhilarating to share in his development and to note his mother's pride and appreciation.

Eventually, Zak got to the age when he was eligible to attend a childcare centre and coincidentally, Jenn had to say goodbye to me and Wee Care too as she and her husband were relocating again. By this time though, because of a lovely picture and write-up of both Jenn and Zak in *Young Parents* magazine, the business had attracted new clients.

One new client was a husband and wife pair who lived in Punggol. Andrew, the husband, would eventually become an investor in Wee Care. Till we sold Wee Care in 2017, he was often forced to bite his tongue and suspend his financial acumen and better knowledge to keep the peace with me! On hindsight, some of my ideas were truly quite idealistic and impractical.

In 1999, Andrew and his wife simply wanted a Baby Buddy to visit baby Samantha every day. She had been born a few months earlier and Andrew's wife, an Ivy League graduate and busy fund manager who worked long hours and travelled frequently, wanted to ensure she was being effectively cared for and engaged with during the workday.

We visited baby Samantha every day for two hours each time. The fees Andrew and his wife paid for these Baby Buddy sessions amounted to one quarter of our monthly revenue at the time! We were indeed a very small and struggling business.

Eventually, we became Baby Buddies to Samantha's siblings, Charles and Anna, too; and slowly, very slowly, over the course of four to five years, more clients came on board. Recruiting effective Baby Buddies who were dedicated and faithful proved to be challenging. There were very few women who wanted to commit themselves to the kind of "babysitting" work the programme was perceived to be doing and I had to agree. A woman could choose to do more glamorous things! Sweating it out while swinging and singing to a baby, bearing backaches from bending and lifting repeatedly, then changing the next nappy while wiping drool or regurgitated milk off our clothes before rushing to the next home carrying bags of toys and other learning resources, was not at all for the faint-hearted. It was incredibly hard work and utterly unfashionable.

What's the point of lipstick and high heels? No one is going to be admiring me today!

But I persisted with the programme knowing that it was for meaningful reasons. For instance, I received feedback from many mothers that they felt more assured knowing that someone was checking on their baby's developmental progress regularly. Babies themselves were thriving and meeting milestones at the right times. These outcomes helped me ride out the occasional bad bumps, especially cruel remarks about why babies needed "tuition" so early in life. Indeed, I found these ideological contestations (misperceptions, perhaps) quite difficult to resolve in my mind at the time. I only knew that there were care and educational needs Wee Care could meet, and I wanted the company to be able to meet those needs in an effective, honest, and respectable manner.

This became even more salient when my former professor and mentor in psychology at the National University of Singapore called me up a few weeks after Jenn and Zak's photograph was published in *Young Parents* magazine.

"What a great programme," she started by saying.

But what about the children with special needs I trained you to work with?

Gulp. I felt an immediate pang of guilt because I knew the needs in this area were even more pressing than the needs of babies and young mothers in Singapore. But I also felt a sense of purpose wash over me. This was something of utmost importance that could and needed to be addressed. More importantly, I could be a part of the solution.

Thus, not long after this conversation, I launched the Home Buddy programme at Wee Care. It was similar to the Baby Buddy programme in that the learning sessions were conducted in the child's home. This time though, the teachers were therapists who had recently graduated with a degree in psychology. I took them in and provided further hands-on training in the principles of Applied Behaviour Analysis (ABA). Applied Behaviour Analysis is often regarded as the "gold standard" approach for children with additional needs, especially Autistic Spectrum Disorders (or ASD, for short). It has been studied since the 1960s and has a large body of empirical, validated research to support its effectiveness.

I will write more about Wee Care's work with special needs children in my next book. Suffice to say for now that when the Home Buddy programme started, we were only one out of two other private centres in Singapore providing the same kinds of learning services.[****] Whilst there were special schools set up and run by the government, there was no dedicated school for children with autism. There was only one small programme accommodating a handful of these students at the Rainbow Centre at Margaret Drive. Moreover, there were no public provisions for children with borderline abilities (that is, children who

---

[****] Over a span of 21 years till 2017, 90% of the children who enrolled in Wee Care for behaviour therapy did so for Autism Spectrum Disorder (ASD); 10% had other developmental issues including Attention-Deficit Hyperactive Disorder (ADHD), Developmental Dyspraxia, Global Developmental Delay and other congenital problems.

fell just outside the range of "average" intelligence but whose abilities did not justify their placement in special schooling). There were also only a handful of speech therapists and occupational therapists in both the public and private spheres. I could have counted them all on my fingers.

More critically, sustaining Wee Care's early intervention programmes was a tough and difficult one throughout my entire tenure in the company. Not only was the recruiting and retaining of therapists a painful and sometimes punishing process, there were also many sociocultural prejudices to cross. For example, children with additional needs were often viewed as "deficient" or "useless". Furthermore, early intervention can never be financially profitable the way other service industries can be. This is because only a small group of children can be served at any one time. Facing huge financial deficits every year on top of the daily challenges of serving the young and vulnerable made for a highly stressful, wearying, and frustrating experience altogether. Indeed, it did not take long for me to realise that the journey I had so excitedly set off on was turning out to be a long trek, both physically and psychologically arduous.

---

15 See for example, Wolins, I. S., Jensen, N. & Ulzheimer, R. (1992). Children's memories of museum field trips: A qualitative study. *The Journal of Museum Education, 17*(2), 17–27.
16 Nelson, K. & Fivush, R. (2004). The emergence of autobiographical memory: A social cultural developmental theory. *Psychological Review, 111*(2), 486–511.
17 This has been best summed in the aphorism, "tune in", "talk more", "take turns". See Suskind, D., Suskind, B., & Lewinter-Suskind, L. (2015). *Thirty million words: Building a child's brain*. New York, NY: Dutton.
18 Sharpe, P. (1993). The national experience in pre-school education. *Teaching and Learning, 13*(2), 67–73. https://repository.nie.edu.sg/handle/10497/1556
19 Department of Statistics Singapore (2019). *Population trends 2019*. [Annual report], Ministry of Trade & Industry, Republic of Singapore. https://www.singstat.gov.sg/-/media/files/publications/population/population2019.pdf

20 Pang, E. F. (1982). *Education, manpower and development in Singapore*. Singapore: Singapore University Press.
21 Goh, C. B. & Gopinathan, S. (2008). The development of education in Singapore since 1965. In S. K. Lee, C. B. Goh, B. Fredriksen, & J. P. Tan (Eds.), *Toward a better future: Education and training for economic development in Singapore since 1965* (pp. 12–38). Washington, D.C.: The World Bank.
22 Liew, M. (2019, April 8). A cultural and economic challenge: Increasing female participation in Singapore's workforce. *ASEAN Today*. https://www.aseantoday.com/2019/04/a-cultural-and-economic-challenge-increasing-female-participation-in-singapores-workforce/
23 Seah, K. C. K. (2019, September 12). Tuition has ballooned to a S$1.4b industry in Singapore. Should we be concerned? *Today Online*. https://www.todayonline.com/commentary/tuition-has-ballooned-s14b-industry-singapore-should-we-be-concerned
24 Wong, A. (2000). *Committee of supply debate FY2000: Senior Minister of State Dr Wong's response to questions on preschool education*. Ministry of Education, Singapore.
25 Ministry of Education. (2010). *Parliamentary reply of 11 January 2010: Nationalise early childhood education*. Ministry of Education, Singapore.
26 Gordon, M. (2002, November 26). *Roots of empathy: Responsive parenting, caring societies*. [Lecture] 1296th Meeting of the Keio Medical Society, Tokyo, Japan. http://www.kjm.keio.ac.jp/past/52/4/236.pdf

BUILDING A SHELTER

An 18th century nursery rhyme from England goes something like this:

> This is the house that Jack built.
> This is the malt that lay in the house that Jack built.
> This is the rat that ate the malt that lay in the house that Jack built.
> This is the cat that chased the rat that ate the malt that lay in the house that Jack built.
> This is the dog that worried the cat that chased the rat that ate the malt that lay in the house that Jack built.

The sequence goes on; much like life, much like what happens when you set out to build something.

I managed Wee Care from home for the first two years because I wanted to be available for Baby 1 and also because I did not have the start-up capital to rent an office and fit it out, plus ... I had no idea if Wee Care would actually succeed. The ideas I had for the business fell outside the usual realm of "tuition", "childcare", and "kindergarten" and it was really not easy for me in the early years to explain what we were about. Even if I eventually found a way to frame it for the listener to understand, there would be quizzical or doubtful looks from the other side about the company's viability in the long run.

Many individuals, now, would not bat an eyelid about running a business from home or working from home, what with the options made available by technological advances these days and a necessity born out of the current Covid-19 pandemic. But in the late 1990s in Singapore, working from home was still something of a second choice. There was little support for it because people generally did not believe that a home business could be a legitimate, credible endeavour. I found myself, time and again, resisting feelings of discouragement whenever the telephone did not ring or fewer people attended a workshop. I felt considerable social pressure too, whenever anyone asked me whether I worked and if yes, where. Somehow, and this could have been my own worrisome nature, Wee Care did not seem to meet social norms for being a valid, justifiable occupation.

In spite of these emotional discomforts, the time eventually arrived when Baby 1 could attend preschool and our Baby Buddy clients turned into toddlers who needed richer social experiences to continue to grow and learn well. I started hunting for commercial space that I could rent and hopefully turn into a small office and playgroup hub. My husband and I really did not have much money at the time, so my choices were limited. I also knew that I needed the office to be close to my mother's home as I would need her support to care for Baby 1 if I had appointments to attend or Baby Buddy, Home Buddy, or playgroup sessions to helm.

I finally found a cosy shop space along Thomson Road. It was next to a car mechanic but I refurbished it nicely, with bright lights, pastel colours, and a clean toilet. A bigger problem was that the shop was shaped like a small, deep cave. It was only 37 square metres from the door to the back wall, which meant that the reception was also the playroom—a tight and tiny square. But it was a start and it made Wee Care seem more convincing ... to me, anyway.

I managed to squeeze a small sofa bed into my office at the back where Baby 1 could have her afternoon naps. I also arranged for the school bus to drop her off at my office when her morning lessons were over. Growth of the business was very slow though, and seriously time- and labour-intensive. It took time to travel to and from homes. It took time to prepare and tidy up after learning sessions. It was also expensive to set aside one Baby Buddy or Home Buddy per child.

To explain: charging $50 an hour for a Baby Buddy session was far **less** income than what we could have earned teaching ten children paying $25 per hour for a playgroup session. But sadly, even our group classes were not cost-effective from a business point of view. Running a playgroup session for two or three toddlers at a time (instead of 15 to 20 children per lesson like what they were doing at the baby gyms and bigger commercial centres) meant that income by the hour was always constrained. Put another way, the economics of covering our overheads like rent, salaries, and teaching resources never ever worked out. Yet, I was still stupidly determined to keep our classes small, cosy, and individualised. Besides, the physical set-up of our centre was far too small to accommodate more children and parents anyhow.

Would I do it again? Probably not in the same form. A few years later, I would learn from Andrew the lessons I missed not studying Economics at A-levels. In 1999 though, I was completely sold on the idea of individualised, high-quality care and education for every child.

Then in 2000, my husband and I welcomed Baby 2, another girl, into our lives.

> From one child + a business;
> to one child, one baby + a business,
> life suddenly became a flurry of non-stop activity.

I would nurse Baby 2 in the morning, get into the office, express breastmilk mid-morning, rush home for lunch and her afternoon feed and to pop the milk bag into the freezer, then get back into the office for afternoon duties before returning home in the evening with another milk bag in tow. At night, I would have Baby 2 close to me so that I could feed her while sleeping.

Inevitably, the stress took its toll. At one point, Baby 2 would wake me at 1:00 a.m. for a feed and I would not be able to fall back to sleep till around 5:00 a.m., only to be roused out of bed again at around 7:00 a.m.

> Like the rain tree holding up thunderstorms
> over you, me, and the ants
> I was fibbed into thinking we could have it all.
> Will the coffee drown the lines of sleep I draw
> around my womanhood and
> the care we all need[27]
> before the lightning hits?

A few months after Baby 2 was born, I heard from the car mechanic that the landlady wanted to raise the rent upon the expiry of the lease. My heart sank. The business was struggling and there was no easy way to increase revenue based on the current operational model to cover the extra funds needed to pay her.

Most start-ups fail, you know.

But I was so stubborn. I came to the conclusion that it was essential for me to look for something else. The new place had to be big enough to serve more children and families, yet affordable enough to keep the business afloat. It had to be in a fairly central location too and according to land regulation laws in Singapore, pre-designated for commercial use.

I searched, I called, I looked, and I prayed. There was not much time because the landlady had cleverly timed her demand a few weeks before the expiry of the lease.

Then a small advertisement in the classifieds caught my eye, something about a shophouse near the Orchard Road area. I asked for a viewing and fell in love with the building. It had high ceilings like most pre-war shophouses in Singapore. The owner had refurbished it for his dot.com company before the bubble burst. The layout included an attic, two large rooms on the second floor, plus two small rooms, and a greenhouse-like room (with clear acrylic panels for a roof) on the first. At the back of the building, smooth granite gravel encircled a deep fish pond which we later drained and covered up to create a backyard for sand- and water-play. I loved it, and made the owner a ridiculous offer.

That's 50% off the asking price!

Well, take it or leave it.

Miraculously, the landlord accepted my offer through the agent. I was elated, then overwhelmed by the task ahead of me. Wee Care would need many, many more students to cover the rent which was now five times more than what we had been required to pay for the unit at Thomson Road.

The building, though, was beautiful and Wee Care operated in it for 10 years. Although there were occasional challenges with its maintenance, we were able to create a clean and wonderful place for our children, teachers, and parents day after day, year after year. It was very hard work, but the returns through the children's joy was immeasurable.

The attic became the teachers' office, which doubled up as a storage space for toys and resources.

We have to start throwing things out. There's too much clutter!

Can you remember where we put the letter cards, the large feely ones?

Denise, the air pump is spoilt. Can you blow into the inflatable rocker?

IKEA became one of our best friends. As the years went by, the storage racks and tubs became increasingly stuffed with learning materials on the verge of falling out, or piling up higgledy-piggledy.

The "greenhouse" became our indoor playground. Because this space was two stories high, I was able to hang long lengths of red, blue, and yellow satin fabric from the second floor down to the opposite wall on the first floor, creating a spectacular visual for all of the children who played in it. Later, I also discovered that we could teach exciting concepts like "high" and "low" by blowing bubbles or throwing confetti down from the second floor into the play space. When we used white confetti, it was like immersing our children in "snow", albeit imaginary.

The bigger room on the second floor became our prominent Open Learning playroom where the learning activities changed at the start of every week according to the theme or children's story we were exploring. Because the playroom was cavernous, we were able to integrate learning into one holistic framework. Hence, if we had read a story about apples, we would cut and taste red and green apples in the sensory area, "harvest" or "sort" apples" like "apple farmers" in the pretend-play areas, paint and print with apple halves at the art-and-craft table, before playing social games like "find the apples" on the main playroom mat. Our children were taught important language, science, and mathematical concepts through play experiences; learning colours, shapes, and everything else that they could—and much more!—in a very happy and secure environment.

In the other large room on the second floor—which was designated the "dining hall" but functioned more like a multipurpose area—we sang and danced, sat in for snacks and/or lunch, and practised life skills such as simple baking and cooking as well as buttoning, lacing and also washing and drying up. Every week incorporated a new inspiration. I found myself buzzing with ideas—and encouraging my team of teachers to create innovative and exciting lessons for our children too.

Wee Care's curriculum developed and improved over time. As toddler playgroup sessions became drop-off pre-nursery classes and—as the children grew older still—nursery and kindergarten level programmes, we added regular outings and "The Project Approach" lessons. We traversed the length and breadth of Singapore visiting parks, gardens, farms, restaurants, museums, the beach, and the theatre. We investigated a myriad of topics—such as cups, chairs, hands, leaves—covering each subject over a period of three months. For the project on hands, we invited an orthopaedics professor to come and speak to the children. He could not spare the time, but he sent two of his medical students with a full human skeleton! We also invited members from the deaf community to come and teach us sign language. Some years later, when exploring drums and percussion instruments, a deaf percussionist in Singapore showed us how she used her sense of touch to "read" the vibrations around her. As teachers, we found we learnt as much as the children did during these very interesting sociocultural and experience-based lessons.

However, as much as I loved how the children were benefitting from our programmes, I was struggling with deeper issues affecting the company. Many years later, while undertaking my Doctoral studies at the Institute of Education in London, I learnt that there are very good and sound reasons why education should not be a commodity that is bought and sold. In Finland, for example, education is considered a public good and a public right. The Finnish government funds education from tax revenue, and the resulting educational system is characterised by equity, quality, and successful student outcomes.[28]

Education run on capitalist lines disrupts accessibility and the equilibrium of opportunity in society because wealthier families can always provide their offspring with more and better learning experiences. What is more, when education lies at the intersection of demand and supply as well as profit and loss, the administrators of the institution will invariably be forced to make decisions that serve financial rather than pedagogical or social ends.[29] I found all of this quite maddening personally and I was also continually shocked at how expensive it was to keep the business afloat, so expensive that I wondered every year whether we would be able to sustain Wee Care for another year. To make things even more psychologically draining, being a "private" entity somehow also meant that the school had to be regulated rather than supported.[30]

Should it not be the case, instead, that teachers expect and count on the support of their government and the wider community to do the work that they have been entrusted with? During my entire watch, Wee Care was continually at the mercy of market forces, landlords, greedy neighbours, and onerous laws and policies. For instance, it had become quite pressing, by 2006, to secure larger premises that would allow Wee Care to be registered as a kindergarten. The options for renting commercial space in Singapore for kindergarten or childcare use, however, had become harder and much more expensive over time. Because of persistent problems caused by parking and noise, it had been deemed that houses in residential areas could not be converted without the explicit agreement of neighbours. While I understood the rationale for this, I was also confronted by the reality that many office and shop spaces lacked green or outdoor space for a garden or a playground. I did not want our children to be in air conditioning all day so I kept looking, with very little success.

The next shock came when our next-door neighbour, who ran a marketing agency, dropped in to speak with me.

"You know," she confided in me, "your landlord is going to terminate your lease."

"Huh? Why?" I was shocked.

"Well, there is the possibility that this whole row of shophouses will be sold en bloc. So, my advice for you is to look for an alternate location as soon as possible."

I was devastated, not only because I loved the building and its location, but also because we were only then just garnering a steady following of families through word-of-mouth recommendations. What is more, I knew that many parents would want their children to attend schools near their homes. Enrolment would drop significantly if Wee Care was forced to move.

But I was equally puzzled as I thought the landlord and I had established a good-enough working relationship to not treat each other distrustfully. After one or two days of fervent prayer, I decided to give the landlord a call to ask if he really intended to terminate our lease. It turned out that, on the contrary, it was my neighbour who had hidden her aims well. She was trying to force the en bloc sale which my landlord was opposed to.

When I did not leave, Ms Neighbour began a threatening campaign, complaining to the traffic police and the Singapore Land Authority (SLA) about the traffic congestion outside our building; a complaint that was categorically untrue because we had never had more than three or four cars parked outside our front door during dismissal, which usually lasted for about fifteen minutes.

Then, she threw the ultimate bombshell on the landlord and I. Because of some archaic land-use law pertaining to the stretch of shophouses along the row that Wee Care was situated in, some shophouses could be used commercially but others only for residential purposes. Which do you think we were operating in? The landlord apologised profusely to me that he had not been aware at the time of his purchase of the property that the premises could not be used commercially. I accepted the apology but it did nothing to relieve my stress. The search for an alternative space was now urgent, but nothing had changed in Singapore: It was still a small country with strict land-use regulations and exorbitant rental rates.

It took about two years, during which time I kept asking the Urban Redevelopment Authority (URA) for an extension of stay at the current premises till we secured another location. The URA was very kind and patient with us but no one was more relieved than I was when we were finally able to move. In this, a Wee Care parent helped to secure space for us in a building that he himself had rented for his own business. Incredibly, the building had a flat roof which we were able to convert into a green roof with funding assistance from the National Parks Board.

Thus, after a protracted wait filled with exceedingly nerve-wracking moments, we had our long sought-after space at last: A bright and inviting reception, 280 square metres of classrooms and a playroom, and more than 460 square metres of outdoor space that we filled with playground equipment, tricycles, and other ride-on vehicles, as well as water inflatables, hula hoops, soccer balls, and other sporting paraphernalia. The site was close to homes, a supermarket, a pharmacy, a hospital, and the Botanic Gardens. It was like a dream come true.

The business challenges, however, persisted. More space meant even more rent—now **eight times more** than what we had paid for the shophouse—which again meant that we had to grow our enrolment quickly if Wee Care was to survive, if not thrive. Hiring continued to be difficult. There remained a short supply of trained and experienced teachers and therapists in Singapore. It seemed to me that no sooner had I trained a teacher or therapist than he or she immediately resigned to move to a new occupation or greener pastures elsewhere. In other words, while we now had what I thought was a solid shelter for our programmes, the wilderness continued to throw many storms our way.

It felt like terrible déjà vu, for instance, when a new tenant moved into the space next to our unit on the main floor. Renovations were conducted without the appropriate health and safety precautions. There were days when our children had to step over cables, pipes, and other kinds of building materials to access our front door, a situation that made me and other safety-conscious parents very upset. Then, I saw a wall come up within a metre of our front door. Apparently, because of feng shui, the new tenant wanted its doors to be built at an angle from ours, which effectively blocked our view of the staircase and anyone's view of us. The narrow corridor between our units was also the result of the landlord maximising the space it was leasing to the new neighbour. It was so confined in width that it could hardly accommodate a stroller and an adult standing next to it.

I was furious but tried to be civil to negotiate a better outcome for Wee Care. The new neighbour, however, was stubborn and arrogant and so was the landlord. In the end, I had no choice. I had to turn to Wee Care parents for help. They responded by mustering up a petition filled with letters of disappointment and disgust.

For days, I felt like a nuclear mushroom cloud had gone up over Wee Care, and things were tense with the neighbour. However, the large-scale and committed protest by all of our amazing parents worked. The wall was cut back, the corridor widened, and our children and staff continued to have visual and physical access to our front door from the building's internal staircase. It was a relief but terribly hard-won. I felt deeply indebted to all of our clients who had stood up for the school. They had gone far beyond their obligations to us as customers.

> The grand old Duke of York, he had ten thousand men;
> He marched them up to the top of the hill,
> And then he marched them down again,
> And when they were up, they were up;
> And when they were down, they were down;
> But when they were only halfway up,
> They were neither up nor down.

I wish I could say that things were peaceful for Wee Care after this incident and well, there was nothing of such insurmountable strain thereafter. But there continued to be rental increases and demands from the authorities to fix this, add that, remove this and reduce that. The building was not managed very well at all; the lift kept breaking down and tenants kept changing, which meant we had to tolerate renovation dust and noise frequently. Once, a new neighbour had a dispute with the landlord and locked the doors of his unit for months, which meant that we were once again denied access to the internal staircase.

Nonetheless, I sought to keep the school as happy a place as possible for our children and families. I also learnt aspects of gardening from a kind gentleman who came to help me with the roof garden once a week. In my mind, the garden symbolised what a wilderness could become, but only with lots of perseverance, attention, and tender, loving care.

---

27 For an excellent exposition on the topic of women's brain, hormonal, and mental health, read Mosconi, L. (2020). *The XX brain: The groundbreaking science empowering women to prevent dementia.* London: Allen & Unwin.

28 For a good overview, read Sahlberg, P. (2011). *Finnish lessons: What can the world learn from educational change in Finland?* New York, NY: Teachers College Press.

29 For a more detailed explanation, read Ball, S. J. (2004, June 17). *Education for sale! The commodification of everything?* [Lecture]. King's Annual Education Lecture 2004, University of London. https://www.researchgate.net/publication/267683502_Education_For_Sale_The_Commodification_of_Everything

30 For a sense of what government regulations are like in the early childhood industry in Singapore these days, see the Early Childhood Development Centre Act 2017 https://sso.agc.gov.sg/Acts-Supp/19-2017/Published/20170511?DocDate=20170511) and the Early Childhood Development Centres Regulations 2018 (https://sso.agc.gov.sg/SL-Supp/S890-2018/Published/20181228?DocDate=20181228).

3

CULTIVATING CURRICULUM

One of the things I enjoy the most about being a teacher is planning and writing up a curriculum. I like it at any level of teaching. In 2019, I worked on a Master's course on early childhood semiotics (the study of signs and symbols and their use or interpretation in the early years) at the Chinese University of Hong Kong (CUHK). While teaching it, I asked my students to analyse an old Michael Jackson video and compare it with a more contemporary BTS video. What was Michael Jackson communicating via his famous dance moves, and how did these compare or contrast with the movements by BTS? More importantly, what do children mean when they move? A pirouette can signify so many things: a dancer, yes; but also, a magician appearing or disappearing; or even, a dolphin or a butterfly. We need to listen to children more than we talk to them, respect their thoughts and ideas more than shunt "facts" into their minds.

In the early days at Wee Care, putting the curriculum together was something I would happily immerse myself into. I could and would plan and write for hours and/or days at a stretch. Cocooned in that head space of ideas and more ideas, I would feel very fulfilled. I would think about my students and how they would respond. I would consider what they would take away with them after the lesson; what they would **construct** in their own minds as knowledge, plus the emotions they were likely to feel in their experience of the session. While not a typical learning objective in the way learning objectives are often described, the elicitation of joy was a feeling I would unconsciously aim for, the kind of joy that jumps up and down, the sort that shines from children's faces and pulsates through musical beats and melodies, infuses through paint and glitter, bubbles, or sand. It is the same kind of joy I might unconsciously think back to long after the event is over; the joy that I usually associate with Christmas, friends, family, fairy lights, and bow-wrapped gifts … the energising and life-giving sort, if you know what I mean.

 The first curriculum I wrote up for Wee Care was the one that was needed for the Baby Buddy Network. It was holistic, covering all of the developmental domains a typical infant should grow and progress through. Under "gross-motor development", for example, I listed and described activities suitable for babies 4 to 6 months old, 7 to 9 months old, 10 to 12 months old, and so on. These included gentle swinging, bilateral exercises, as well as techniques to support and encourage cruising. The guidelines and informational materials for each developmental quarter were then bound in thin volumes that I would distribute to the individual Baby Buddy teachers according to their specific caseloads. From a photo software programme, I downloaded a cheerful Teddy Bear image that we subsequently reproduced on the cover page of each volume. Even now, whenever I chance upon this image in the salvaged copies of curriculum I have in my book cupboard, I cannot help but smile.

The next curriculum I had to put together was the one that eventually became an important component in all Wee Care schools and programmes, Open Learning. To me, Open Learning was a coherent interpretation and application of some of the most eminent theories in child psychology and education. From Jean Piaget, for example, the curriculum incorporated the principle that children have an intrinsic desire to learn, a drive to make sense of the environment. Hence, the Open Learning playroom allowed the children to interact with objects, situations, and each other, and not sit passively in front of teachers to absorb knowledge as if they were "sponges". According to Piaget's framework, as children experience and enact their ideas within the physical environment, they form schemas of understanding that are more meaningful and permanent than ideas acquired by simply memorising material presented by others.[31]

Another well-known psychologist, Jerome Bruner, suggested that "any subject can be taught in some intellectually honest form to any child at any stage of development" so long as basic ideas are revisited and built upon.[32] Lessons should encourage intuition and novelty, to keep students motivated and active.[33] Later, Bruner described the process of learning to be similar to the construction of a skyscraper. A scaffold is needed to enable new understandings to develop from earlier concepts. What this means, in practice, is that whether in the classroom or in parent-child interactions, it is the adult who provides assistance that is carefully adjusted to the child's or learner's needs.[34]

This aspect of Bruner's theory extends from Lev Vygotsky's idea of the Zone of Proximal Development (or ZPD), where learners can achieve a new, "potential" level of development (beyond the level that they can already achieve on their own) with the help of others.[35] Or, as Vygotsky described it, "what the child is able to do in collaboration today he will be able to do independently tomorrow".[36]

In combination, Piaget's, Vygotsky's, and Bruner's theories significantly influenced the way I thought about learning and teaching. They were so essential to what and how I wanted young children to learn that I made sure the principles were diffused through our day-to-day practices at Wee Care, and applied consistently. Open Learning was thus a pedagogical approach that combined these principles into a coherent whole, an approach that educationalists have described as "open education" or "discovery learning". This approach is often distinguished by seven key features. They include open space, materials to manipulate, multi-age grouping, active participants and learners, individualised instruction, diagnostic evaluation, and team teaching.

Explained in more detail, the open education classroom is very spacious. It is usually divided into separate learning areas by screens, bookcases, or rugs of different colours. Seating arrangements are very flexible. Children can move around and the teachers can work with them individually, in pairs, or in small groups. Children from different age groups may be placed in the same Open Learning class too. At Wee Care, we tended to combine the two- and three-year-olds into one group, and the five- and six-year-olds into another group. Children from all age groups would have music and movement at the same time. In this way, the younger students in the school could learn from their older schoolmates, and in turn, the older students could practise important socio-emotional skills such as having empathy and/or being patient with their younger peers.

Open education typically also requires diverse materials in the different learning areas in the room. At Wee Care, we had a space for sensory investigations, pretend play, art and craft, as well as group games. In each area, and within the allotted times, the children would be encouraged to be active participants in their own learning. They could select the materials that they wished to work or play with, make suggestions, and determine their own pace of learning—which might sometimes mean walking away from something that they were no longer interested in doing. The teacher was thus only a resource person to facilitate learning, not a fearsome authority figure.

As a result of this ethos, learning at Wee Care took on a far more child-centred tone overall. The pace and methods used were always based on the needs and abilities of the individual students. Moreover, because Open Learning necessitated team teaching (more teachers were required to attend to the smaller groups operating in the playroom at any one time), it became possible for more in-depth and naturalistic observations of the children. This meant that diagnostic evaluations of their progress and/or needs could be undertaken simultaneously, but also, discreetly and sensitively in a non-judgemental and non-threatening manner.

Personally, I discovered that the most interesting and informative observations of children in the Open Learning playroom centred around their creativity, language, play abilities, and temperament or socio-emotional skills. A child might pick up a stick, for instance, and use it as a racquet. If this observation was supported by other observations of the child initiating physical play with other resources in the environment, we might conclude that the child had a kinaesthetic preference to learning. Or we might note that his skills in eye-hand coordination had developed significantly in the past three months or so. Sometimes, we might observe other sorts of behaviours; such as the child inviting his peers to use the same stick to play a modified form of rounders, verbally negotiating the rules of the game with these mates and/or changing the rules if a peer disagreed. This might constitute other traits or abilities that we would then note down in the child's biannual progress report, such as a friendly personality, enhanced conversational skills, or an increased capacity to engage in complex problem-solving within a social group. Open Learning was, in this way, a window of many panels that afforded the teachers and I fascinating glimpses into the hearts and minds of our students each time.

Meta-analyses[37] have shown that open education programmes facilitate stronger self-concepts, levels of creativity and positive feelings towards school. In particular, it is the child-centred aspects of the model, along with its individualised, diagnostic approach of teaching and the provision of manipulative materials that accrue these benefits. Once, when we were in the desperate midst of looking for new premises to move into, I shared with a Wee Care mother that it was difficult finding affordable commercial space in Singapore that would allow me to retain the original size of our Open Learning playroom, the one that was the highlight of our Orchard Road site. She expressed genuine disappointment and said that her children would be so sad about its loss.

The playroom is their life.

Indeed, Open Learning evoked so much joy, discovery, and innumerable possibilities for open-ended play for all of the children and teachers alike that I did everything within my power to ensure that we had a playroom at the new location and in every Wee Care centre thereafter, even when it meant paying more rent for more space. Open Learning proved so successful as a system of learning through the years that even our early intervention therapists would seek to use the playroom for their therapy sessions once their students were ready to access the large expanse of learning opportunities. We also wove segments of Open Learning into our weekly social skills playgroup programme. It proved to be hugely popular, not just with the special children but their parents as well, who saw how much their children enjoyed learning and connecting with their peers and teachers. Indeed, the set-up became an intrinsically fun and motivating platform for the development of the children's skills in social language, social thinking, and social play.

Unsurprisingly, Open Learning became such an integral part of life at Wee Care that it was incorporated into every Holiday Programme where, during these special weeks, themes in the playroom would change almost daily. It was hard work designing and creating the scenes and pulling all of the resources together. The typical workflow would look something like this:

- Teacher drafts the Open Learning lesson plan, based on the story being featured.
- Senior teacher or principal checks and approves the draft.
- All drafts sent to Denise for a final check.
- Finalised lesson plans sent to the resource teacher.
- Resource teacher designs and plans the various learning areas, including the scenes for imaginary play.
- Resource teacher—with assistance from junior teachers, assistant teachers, interns, or volunteers, and sometimes even the managers—makes the materials needed for the learning areas (e.g. picture cards, wall designs, props for pretend).

- On Mondays (set-up days), the entire playroom is transformed. What was a scene from a French café the previous week, replete with imaginary French croissants and other delectable pastries, might now be the moon and outer space!

Needless to say, Open Learning lesson plans for an academic term or Holiday Programme would take a few weeks to turn into a reality. So planning would often happen long before the actual lessons took place. Understandably, our expenses for Open Learning were very high, but the returns—both educational and in goodwill—were invaluable. Specifically, there were so many positive outcomes; our students, for one, were happy and confident. Many made the transition to primary school without difficulty. Many entered the gifted education programme later in life. We graduated many special needs students into local and international mainstream schools too.

We were, however, not unaffected by naysayers, especially in the early years of Wee Care's existence. Some of these naysayers were competitors who had a commercial and ideological axe to grind with our school. It used to annoy me to no end when they would call on pretext and ask about our "philosophy of teaching". Their questions would be vastly different from an interested parent's enquiry (which would usually revolve around programme times, what to pack for snack or lunch, how to manage separation anxiety, what to do with toileting issues, the school's allergy precautions, etc.). Once, responding over the phone about our teaching framework, I heard laughter in the background of the call, a smothered laugh from the caller, and the patronising words, "Oh yes, of course, I understand, Denise, I understand perfectly." You can imagine how riled I was, and yet, I had no choice but to be polite and continue answering her questions—as briefly as possible!

Another time, I received an email from a competitor who was responding to my termly newsletter article, "It's Not About Flashcards!" In response to this educational fad at the time, I had written: "Flashcards should only form part of a more comprehensive early development programme that encourages peer interaction (social skills) and creative thought (cognitive skills) through activities that incorporate a shared focus, discovery, exploration, experimentation, problem-solving, and playing pretend." I had also outlined some of the dangers of precocious reading. These included the accessing of information beyond the child's emotional maturity to make sense of; the irrelevance of knowing some names (e.g. of classical musicians) without using these names in meaningful conversation; an emphasis on verbal labelling to the exclusion of other pragmatic language functions (such as requesting, describing, asking, and taking perspective); the dogmatism that there is only one correct answer (Mozart is Mozart, right?), and the ethos of continued testing faced by the child.

I am not sure how many parents at the time I managed to convince, but putting my thoughts to words in these regular newsletters helped me (or so I hoped) explain why we taught the way we did, and why we did not teach the way some thought we should teach! Strangely, the competitor took advantage of these "flashcards" points to segue into a completely different pedagogical model, that of Maria Montessori. He outlined why Montessori's method was far superior to any other method and probably expected me to respond and agree. Or maybe he had a different reason for writing; maybe he just wanted to tell me that his school was better than Wee Care. Thankfully, I had the restraint not to reply because the discussion would not have been productive at all. I was still young and feisty and would have tried to punch him out in a concentrated debate.

Over the ensuing years, I saw the rise and fall of many "types" of preschools in Singapore. In the early 2010s, the Reggio Emilia approach became popular and was touted to be the "better" way for young children to learn. Preschools espousing the Reggio way emerged, some schools rebranded, and teachers were invited to visit Italy where they could see the pedagogy enacted in its natural context.

Ironically, and somewhat incongruous to its popularity, the proponents of Reggio Emilia have said that their approach is not easily transferable. There are historical, cultural, and environmental factors that allow the Reggio method to maintain its true, effective, and sustainable form.[38] Without these elements, it may be more valid to consider the school as being Reggio-inspired than authentically Reggio, or one that implements the Reggio approach.[39]

Now, I am not saying this to spite the Reggio framework or preschools that have decided to adopt its philosophical underpinnings. I am not dismissive of Maria Montessori's model or other early childhood frameworks like Forest School, Waldorf, or HighScope either. Rather, I have learnt that each of these approaches provides us with a slice of the truth. Each of these models communicates **some** truth about what effective early childhood learning should be or look like.

From Maria Montessori, for instance, I have learnt that children can organise themselves and learn independently through the use of self-correcting materials.[40] At the same time, I have appreciated the importance that Forest School gives to outdoor activities, and often wished that I had had the chance to enjoy such experiences myself when growing up.⁴¹ In contrast, HighScope is a very structured system that allows for close monitoring of a child's learning, especially in the more academic domains of literacy and numeracy.⁴² This can be invaluable in the later preschool years when the teacher has to be mindful of the child's eventual transition to primary school, especially in a country like Singapore! Last but not least, Reggio Emilia has reminded me that children can communicate in many different ways; that we should respect and, where possible, encourage the expression of their ideas through varying modalities.⁴³ In fact, Reggio has inspired more formative (rather than summative) evaluations of young children's development and progress by encouraging regular and systematic documentation of their work, including photographs of the children engaged in their projects as well as comments and transcripts of conversations. Personally, I find that the emphasis the model places on visual aesthetics to be both joyful and calming.⁴⁴

More importantly, though, when one compares and contrasts these models, one realises that it is not possible for any one preschool to incorporate **every distinguishing element every day** from each of these systems. It is simply not practically and philosophically feasible. There are constraints of space, time, and worldview. For instance, the Reggio classroom is actually an atelier—a creative studio. The use of structured Montessori materials in such a space would be anathema to the creativity and freedom-of-expression that the Reggio framework passionately advocates. Yet, we also know that the Montessori method yields very successful outcomes for its students, both academic and non-academic.⁴⁵

Likewise, the weight given to more academic forms of learning in the HighScope system would run counter to the spirit of adventure, exploration, and discovery promoted by Forest Schools. But

HighScope tracks learning across 58 key developmental indicators (KDIs), an asset to teachers who want or need a comprehensive evaluation system for their students.[46] Who is to say that one approach is the undisputed winner, hands-down? Rather, we need to value the principles afforded by each of these learning approaches and remind ourselves, as teachers and/or parents, that a child needs every facet of opportunity in his/her life, in varying measure, to:

>run, jump, swim, climb, sit
>read, write
>
>be creative,
>expressive
>
>try, experiment,
>explore, discover, imagine
>
>learn but also,
>
>walk in the rain
>play with friends
>be puzzled
>ask questions
>
>listen
>think
>dream
>
>and be true

When we have done so, we will probably be closer to having arrived at the "right" curriculum for the child. We will probably have realised, as well, that every effective and meaningful curriculum must accommodate the individual child's needs, temperament, and style of learning. Keeping one's eyes on all of these aspects, however, can be a real challenge to any early childhood educator and, indeed, was a balancing act for all of us at Wee Care too.

---

31 For an easy primer about Jean Piaget's theories, read Singer, D. G., & Revenson, T. A. (1996). *A Piaget primer: How a child thinks (Rev. ed.)*. New York, NY: Plume.
32 Bruner, J. S. (1960). *The process of education: A landmark in educational theory*. Cambridge, MA: Harvard University Press.
33 For more information about Jerome Bruner's theories, see Takaya, K. (2013). *Jerome Bruner: Developing a sense of the possible*. Dordrecht, the Netherlands: Springer.
34 Bruner, J. S. (1975). From communication to language: A psychological perspective. *Cognition, 3*(3), 255–287.
35 Vygotsky, L. S. (1978). Interaction between learning and development (M. Lopez-Morillas, Trans.). In M. Cole, V. John-Steiner, S. Scribner, & E. Souberman (Eds.), *Mind in society: The development of higher psychological processes* (pp.79–91). Cambridge, MA: Harvard University Press.
36 Vygotsky, L. S. (1987). Thinking and speech (N. Minick, Trans.). In R. W. Rieber, & A. S. Carton (Eds.), *The collected works of L. S. Vygotsky: Vol. 1. Problems of general psychology* (pp. 39–285). New York: Plenum Press. (Original work published 1934).
37 Giaconia, R. M., & Hedges, L. V. (1982). Identifying features of effective open education. *Review of Educational Research, 52*(4), 579–602.
38 Follari, L. (2015). *Foundations and best practices in early childhood education: History, theories and approaches to learning* (3rd ed.). Upper Saddle River, NJ: Pearson.
39 Stremmel, A. J. (2012). A situated framework: The Reggio experience. In N. File, J. J. Mueller, & D. B. Wisneski (Eds.), *Curriculum in early childhood education: Re-examined, rediscovered, renewed* (pp. 133–145). New York, NY: Routledge.
40 Montessori, M. (2014). *The Montessori Method*. New Brunswick, NJ: Transaction Publishers.
41 O'Brien, L. (2009). Learning outdoors: The Forest School approach. *International Journal of Primary, Elementary and Early Years Education, 37*(1), 45–60. https://www.tandfonline.com/doi/full/10.1080/03004270802291798
42 Michael-Luna, S., & Heimer, L. G. (2012). Creative curriculum and HighScope curriculum: Constructing possibilities in early education. In N. File, J. J. Mueller & D. B. Wisneski (Eds.), *Curriculum in early childhood education: Re-examined, rediscovered, renewed* (pp. 120–132). New York, NY: Routledge.

43   Edwards, C. P., Gandini, L., & Forman, G. E. (1993). *The hundred languages of children: The Reggio Emilia approach to early childhood education*. Norwood, NJ: Ablex Publishing Corporation. Also, see Kang, J. (2007). How many languages can Reggio children speak? Many more than a hundred! *Gifted Child Today, 30*(3), 45–65.
44   Tarr, P. (2001). Aesthetic codes in early childhood classrooms: What art educators can learn from Reggio Emilia. *Art Education, 54*(3), 33–39.
45   Lillard, A., & Else-Quest, N. (2006). The early years: Evaluating Montessori education. *Science, 313*(5795), 1893–1894.
46   Follari, L. (2015). *Foundations and best practices in early childhood education: History, theories and approaches to learning* (3rd ed.). Upper Saddle River, New Jersey: Pearson.

4
WELCOMING NEW LIFE

It was significant that the years of Wee Care's infancy coincided with my own children's early years. It made everything that happened at work or within my home relevant to the other. Parents, for instance, would ask me about behavioural strategies that had worked for my girls. In turn, they would keep me updated about the latest news in town, such as upcoming theatre performances or whether this-school-or-that-school had had a viral outbreak and, more importantly, that Wee Care had to be extra, extra careful not to allow a similar outbreak to occur on its premises.

At another level, places that I had visited with my children over the weekend became ideas for field trips. Holidays that we had taken as a family or books that I had bought for my own children became sources of inspiration for curricula or author themes. We had fabulous terms exploring the stories of Mem Fox, Pamela Allen, Leo Lionni, and Eric Carle. We journeyed imaginatively through Australia and Africa, learnt about the alphabet reading *Chicka Chicka Boom*

Boom,[47] played with *Alfie Out of Doors*,[48] then ran to the beach to examine *Flotsam*[49] and jellyfish.

It seemed like there was never a time when I was not breathing, thinking, or dreaming babies and children. Predictably, my children's classmates became their friends but their parents, my clients, became my friends too. There was much to talk about, discuss, and organise over the children's play dates, shared rides, sleepovers, birthdays, and other joint experiences.

There was another aspect to this parallel timeline. I wanted Baby 2 to continue attending Wee Care if she could and not attend another preschool elsewhere. I could not, frankly, find another kindergarten at the time that met my standards for quality care and attention. Even the higher-end, upmarket preschools seemed cold and unfriendly. Hence, there were both commercial and personal reasons why Wee Care's maturing as a business correlated with the age groups we served (first babies, then toddlers and finally, preschoolers). I had a vested interest to ensure that curricula extensions were done progressively and successfully, mainly by developing an extra year of more advanced lessons on top of an earlier year so that Baby 2 and her friends' (the pioneering cohort's) increasing developmental, especially cognitive, needs could be met. In this way thus, Wee Care "grew with" its students, and wonderfully, the kindergarten was fully operational by the time Baby 3 needed it.

It was a lovely feeling to be able to share time and space with my girls at work. I think this is why childcare facilities that are built within office buildings are so valued and needful. A woman does not stop being a mother when she leaves for work, especially when that work involves caring for or educating the children of other mothers! I also think that this is one of the reasons why some workplace cultures are more successful than others. Those that value their female employees by allowing them a no-questions-asked flexibility communicate a deep respect that a woman will not underappreciate, not when she knows how long and hard the road to emancipation has been.

Two of my girls are now adults and the youngest a teenager. I sometimes think of the messages they might have imbued watching me work. They had a privileged gaze certainly, because they were able to call me "Mummy" while others used the respectful address, "Teacher Denise".

Here's a funny story for you, Denise. Jack said Baby 3 is confused. I asked him why. He said she is confused because she keeps calling Teacher Denise, "Mummy." I told him she was right. You are her mummy. His face said it all. It was like the rug had been pulled from under his feet!

My god-daughter, Ling, who attended Wee Care too, would claim her privilege in a different way. In the mornings, she would wait decisively till after the whole school had chorused, "Good morning, Teacher Denise" before piping up at the very end, "God-Ma". There would be a round of laughter from the teachers, and I would smile in acknowledgement at her sweet innocence. But I would also feel obliged to refocus everyone's attention back quickly on the day ahead so that no one would feel left out. It did surprise me, at the time, though how early we humans begin to make sense of abstract notions like in-group status, and how it contributes to our developing social identities and self-esteem.[50]

But what of my own social identity? I did have a privileged status at Wee Care certainly—but only later when we were no longer a rookie start-up. From day one, I had been a working mother, bearing the load of my multiple roles and responsibilities on an intense day/

night schedule for years. Returning to employment—albeit self-employment—after one year of being a stay-at-home mother to Baby 1 incurred what I now realise were significant psycho-emotional costs. It had been difficult leaving the baby with other caregivers, however loving and responsive they were. The accusatory thought that my daughter would grow up to be an emotionally impaired person because of my frequent absences was almost relentless. Indeed, although I had resolved to be an **available** mother **all of the time**, reality struck when one baby became two babies and then three, and over time, a whole school (and more) of other parents' babies.

Sociologists have pointed to the paradoxical biases faced by working mothers where they are perceived as being less committed to both motherhood **and** work. Put simply, "I am a bad mother" (while at work) and "a not-so-good employee" (when tending to home needs). A re-socialisation process is often required for the mother to realign her professional self with her maternal self.[51] For me, guilt became an all-too-familiar emotion during this process, an unwelcome friend signalling my selfishness at wanting independence and a career, an identity outside of the one naturally ascribed by my wifehood and motherhood. Not every woman experiences this guilt, I know, and some may simply choose to ignore it for very sound economic reasons. Of the ones assailed by self-reproach, I proffer that they probably cope with the remorse by "making it up" to their children in other ways. I will be the first to admit that I tried everything, from toys and food to weekend jaunts and long holidays. I even allowed my children to climb into our bed at night, an absolute "no-no" in (Western) expert circles.[52]

One mother-client was so appalled when she learnt I had succumbed to co-sleeping with the baby that she chided me sternly for it.

"And what would you advise other parents to do?" I remember her saying.

It was like I had lost my badge of honour; that I should have taken GUILT and stared it down, not capitulated so easily and worse, retain my role as a respected parent advisor while struggling with issues of my own. To her, it was nothing short of hypocrisy.

"Women are very good at making themselves feel guilty," a lovely lady professor once said to me.

"Touché," I thought, "and each other."

Some scholars have sought to rationalise negative emotions such as maternal guilt by busting what they describe as "the motherhood myth". This myth portrays an idealised image of mothers, a biased view that emphasises maternal devotion without taking into account the evidence that different mothers exercise their motherhood in different ways, for example, by utilising different maternal strategies and cooperative child-rearing arrangements. Instead, according to this myth, mothers should be exclusive caretakers who are universally present, nurturing, and kind—not absent, selfish, or aggressive.[53]

I did have my own "maternal strategies" and arrangements for childcare. My mother, for one, was a very involved grandmother. She had been a working mother herself. For 30 years, she had been the Night Sister at the maternity ward of a well-respected not-for-profit hospital in Singapore. When I started Wee Care, it coincided with her time to retire from nursing. But she was reluctant to stop working. She had enjoyed her social freedoms and financial independence for so long. I cajoled her to step back from the night shifts and heavy responsibilities by saying that she could still be productive helping out at Wee Care. Little did I know then that she would become an integral part of the preschool as a supporting member of staff, staying well beyond my tenure, long after I had left.

"Why are you still working here?" I remember asking her when she was already in her seventies and yet the first to appear at school every morning. We could always count on her to open the doors and be there to receive the early drop-offs.

"Once a mother, always a mother," she would reply quietly but pointedly.

Given her background in nursing, it seemed natural to me that Wee Care should provide midwifery services in the early years as one of its core offerings (although this aspect of the company's services was eventually replaced by educational programmes; the latter being my preferred area of interest and expertise). My mother dutifully visited new mothers at home to advise them on newborn bathing and caring techniques. She ran training sessions for parents and domestic helpers too.

Later, and in spite of her advancing years, my mother would care for anxious toddlers, organise and re-organise cupboards and storage areas with a tenacious vengeance, help with the making of learning resources—cutting, pasting, or wrapping things neatly—and generally just encouraging the staff whenever they were discouraged or under the weather. She would come to tell me whenever there were problems the staff were attempting to hide, knowing that it would be good for issues to be resolved promptly. My mother was such a popular feature at Wee Care that to this day, whenever I meet former staff or clients along the street or in a restaurant, many will ask about her.

In the afternoons, Auntie Lisa (as she was affectionately known) would leave a little earlier to travel to my home and spend a few hours with my girls. She would keep an eye on the baby or toddler, and read or play with the older one(s). Her presence went a long way in assuaging my guilt at not being home early enough or not being present when this child or that child was sick, as did regular visits from my children's other grandmother, my mother-in-law. Together, both mothers helped me grapple with the new lives I had birthed, and with the invariable busyness these entailed. They seemed to understand, more than me perhaps, what motherhood really means. It is a journey of absolute devotion and sacrifice.

Once a mother, always a mother.

Thank you, Mummy xx

Motherhood helped me understand the perspectives of other mothers at Wee Care too; their aspirations and concerns, joys and fears. It created a cradle of empathy—if you could call it that—from which I could draw insights and ideas for programmes and strategies. I was not always successful, certainly, but I would like to think there was a sisterhood (perhaps?) to our shared motherhood.

But even sisters disagree.

One memory sticks out in my mind especially. Every year, Wee Care would organise a celebration for Mothers' Day and Fathers' Day. We would try to find an appropriate activity that we thought most parents would enjoy. Unfortunately, we ended up quite often resorting to gender-stereotypical ideas for the mothers versus the fathers.

To illustrate; mothers were treated once or twice to a Wee Care "spa" where their children were encouraged to give them back, head, shoulder, and hand massages—"as a sign of your love and appreciation for Mummy," we told them. On the day of the celebration, gamelan music would tinkle softly in the background and the smell of scented candles would waft sweetly from every classroom. Mothers would receive orchids and be invited to lie down on gym mats, eyes covered with cool cucumber slices, for a relaxing 10 minutes. Another time, we treated the mothers to a "hair makeover" experience—again, with the children spritzing and combing. The year before I left, all of the mothers worked on a batik sarong which we auctioned off (to Dr Lin Zhaoru, a scientist and Wee Care mother, no less!) for charity (to Syrian refugee children specifically, if my memory serves me right).

And the fathers? Well, they had exciting adventures like an Amazing Race down Orchard Road, a visit to the dinosaur exhibit at the Singapore ArtScience Museum, and one year, a visit to a farm in Johor, Malaysia! It was all very exciting compared to the calming and soothing activities we picked for our mothers.

This, however, did not seem correct to me at all, so one year, I was determined that the gender bias should be reversed. I told the teachers we would organise an Amazing Race for the mothers, but through Gardens by the Bay. The Wee Care staff seemed fairly keen to make it happen, so preparations went underway. Who would have guessed the "disaster" that happened? Some mothers were so resolute about winning that they upset their teammates (and the mothers in other teams) in the process. Some mothers hated getting hot and sweaty. When they arrived at the finish line, they showed their displeasure by frowning and glaring at me. It was such a disappointing outcome that I never attempted to hold a competition for mothers on Mothers' Day ever again. To be honest, the same (but milder) disquiet had happened when we had organised a fashion competition with teams of mothers constructing an outfit from recyclable materials.

Surely, we cannot give prizes to everyone? I had reasoned.

But I should have learnt quickly. Around the same time, we had also organised a dance experience and informed the mothers we would recognise the best-dressed mother-child pairs at the close of the celebration. One mother got so upset at not having won that I felt terrible afterwards. To ease my guilt at having been the cause of her disappointment, I bought an extra prize and gave it to her the next day.

I know better now.

Women need care too.

There is something in and about motherhood that yearns for rest, appreciation, and recognition. I really should have known better. But I can smile at these memories knowing that they taught me something about human nature and the extent of the empathy we must cultivate as early childhood educators towards our children and their families.

I also know, in hindsight, that they were part of the new life we were grappling with as a school. The more our enrolment grew, the more diverse our clientele became. With this diversity came a wide range of varied perspectives and worldviews, some of which I was not always able to anticipate.

There were trying moments in particular, moments of high stress for the child, parent, and teachers. One such event—a milestone really—was the toddler's introduction to being dropped off at school for the first time. Much of the evidence from developmental research tells us that it is normal for children to experience separation anxiety during this phase.[54] It is stranger if the child does not react at all. After all, as I would say to the equally anxious parent, "You have looked after your child from birth. He knows and trusts you."

Some mothers, however, understandably stressed at hearing their child cry, would berate me for being mean and/or "forcing" the child to attend school on their own; this in spite of the family's preparation beforehand in the parent-toddler playgroup programme, sometimes for six months or longer. The gentler mothers would cry themselves, which at least allowed me to assure them with photographs or videos that their child was fine after the first few minutes of tears. It was not easy back then, without the use of smartphones, to take photographs or videos. But we put ourselves through the tedious process of documentation and communication anyway, burning the final images or video footage on shiny CDs, the extra time spent a labour of love for the child and mother.

One intrepid mother comes to mind here. It was the early 2000s and she was very concerned about her son who had mild learning needs. To check that he was adjusting to the programme, she decided she would crawl into Wee Care on all fours so as not to be spotted. I found her when I rounded a corner and almost fell over her.

As a school, we devised all sorts of strategies to alleviate the children's (and their parents') stress. I wrote a three-page essay describing what might happen in the first few days of school. This included a list of Dos and Don'ts which would be handed out to parents before the big day. The Dos included giving the child something to hold on to that communicated, "Mummy will be back to pick you up", usually a personal belonging such as a wristwatch or a soft toy. Don'ts included refraining from saying things like, "Yes, she is such a naughty teacher, right, for taking you from me?" You will be surprised how many mothers used this line. I had to explain to these parents that they were basically communicating to their child that the teacher was evil and/or to be feared. Now, why would any child want to leave her mother for a person like that? Instead, I would emphasise how important it was that the mother should convey trust and affirmation that the child would be in very good hands while in school.

In spite of all of these assurances though, separation anxiety continued to be one of the main stress points for all of our families and teachers throughout my entire time at Wee Care. By the end of my tenure, I had implemented a new policy that a child would spend progressively longer chunks of time in school during the first few weeks of him/her starting sessions. The first two or three days might be for just half an hour, increasing to an hour, then longer still, over the entire transition period which might last a few weeks. But it definitely helped to reduce the child's anxiety and, correspondingly, the parents and teachers too.

Unfortunately, this "phased introduction" did result in some parents arguing that they were being required to pay for the full three-hour session for the day when only a half-hour or hour would be utilised. It was another instance of money befuddling the good intentions we had set out to achieve on behalf of the child and family. Indeed, this suspicion of a profit agenda made it difficult at times to earn a parent's trust, with unpleasant consequences sometimes over seemingly trivial matters (e.g. lessons ending five minutes before schedule). It is probably the saddest lesson I have learnt running preschools. Money enables teachers and schools to do what they do. There is a direct relationship, in fact, between the amount of funding available to a school and the quality of the lessons (and teachers) the school can provide. The money motive, however—whether real or imagined—can alternately disable and disrupt everything that is meaningful in early childhood education: relationships, connection, care, and—dare I say it?—love.

---

47   Martin, B., Jr., & Archambault, J. (1989). *Chicka Chicka Boom Boom*. New York, NY: Beach Lane Books.
48   Hughes, S. (1992). *The Big Alfie Out of Doors Storybook*. London: The Bodley Head.
49   Wiesner, D. (2006). *Flotsam*. New York, NY: Clarion Books.
50   For a research study illustrating this, see Nesdale, D., & Flesser, D. (2001). Social identity and the development of children's group attitudes. *Child Development, 72*(2), 506–517. https://srcd.onlinelibrary.wiley.com/doi/epdf/10.1111/1467-8624.00293
51   Ladge, J. J., & Greenberg, D. N. (2015). Becoming a working mother: Managing identity and efficacy uncertainties during resocialization. *Human Resource Management, 54*(6), 977–998.
52   Both the American Academy of Pediatrics (AAP) and the UK's National Health Service (NHS) strongly discourage co-sleeping. For a summary of the controversy, please see Carter, M. (2020, July 7). *Co-Sleeping: The pros and cons of a family bed*. Parents. https://www.parents.com/baby/sleep/co-sleeping-the-pros-and-cons-of-the-family-bed/
53   Rotkirch, A., & Janhunen, K. (2009). Maternal guilt. *Evolutionary Psychology, 8*(1), 90–106. https://journals.sagepub.com/doi/pdf/10.1177/147470491000800108
54   Bowlby, J. (1960). Separation anxiety: A critical review of the literature. *The Journal of Child Psychology and Psychiatry, 1*(4), 251–269.

5

CARING, MOTHERING, LOVING, TEACHING

Love is a difficult word. From my experience, many parents would like their children to be loved by their teachers, especially their first, earliest teachers. But they would never dare ask for, expect, or assume it is possible in the context of schooling. After all, teachers are teachers. They play a role for a season of time before the child moves on to a new teacher in a different classroom (or school) when the next academic year begins.

Love? Love is a complicated thing, and love complicates things.

In *Teaching with Love*, Lisa Goldstein describes the dilemma for teachers like this, "... relationship is a given, caring is fine, affection and fondness are acceptable, but love steps over the line."[55] Indeed, to many, infusing love in one's teaching risks the unprofessional, and hence is unnecessary, even objectionable. Teachers, according to these cynics, cannot genuinely love their students.[56]

Yet, for those who teach young children, love is at the very heart and soul of their days and nights. Just ask any early childhood educator. They may not use the word "love" when describing what they do or feel. But it is there. They are teachers who "care so deeply and love so much".[57]

This love, according to Goldstein, is "teacherly love", and extends from the belief that each child has a right to be loved and understood in his/her school setting.[58]

I had always assumed it was important to love children, more so if they were mine, and certainly needful if I had been entrusted with the responsibility to look after them. Perhaps it was the way I had been mothered (parented) and grand-mothered (grand-parented) myself. Or maybe it was just a simple assumption borne out of my Christian faith, a faith that had heard it uttered many times, "Let the little children come to me," to Love.[59]

But the notion of love in teaching, admittedly, is problematic for many reasons. For one, while many teachers in the early years do love their students, we cannot and should not expect that all will. Most will be prompted by a desire to serve and effect positive change in the next generation, but not all will be comfortable with the notion of loving a child the same way one would love one's own child. Indeed, as much as I have loved—and still love—my former students, it would be dishonest (and wrong) of me to claim that I have loved, or love, my own children less.

And yet, mothering facilitated my life as a teacher and teaching augmented my abilities as a mother.[60] Over time, most of my responses at home or in school were conflated, automatic reactions of a hybrid nature, part and parcel of my subconscious thoughts, ways of perceiving and eventual decision-making.

Tantrum? Stay cool.

Fever? Hydrate, medicate.

Sharp furniture edge? Stick on a baby guard.

Picky eater? Bake the veggies in cake.

Quarrelling children? Mediate and reward individual efforts at collaboration.

Bored, unmotivated child?

Set up a tent.
Get out the cardboard.
Pull out the books.
Pump up the volume.
Put on a show.
Make a mess.
Make pictures.
Make cookies.
Make play dough shapes.
Make bubbles.
Have fun. Laugh,
and laugh some more.

There are definite overlaps between teaching and mothering. In fact, some studies have shown that the qualities associated with being a "good mother" and a "good teacher" are almost identical.[61]

But there are also clear differences.⁶²

A mother's responsibilities are diffuse and limitless. She wakes at night, she cooks, she cleans, she cuddles, she cries. The teacher's obligations are justifiably more specific and limited.

The mother-child bond is emotionally intense. The relationship between the child and the teacher less so.

The mother is free to be spontaneous. She is her own authority, her own boss. The teacher must be planful, careful, and rational.

The mother cares for her own family. The teacher is responsible for many children and invariably, their families.

The mother is partial. The teacher must be impartial.

The mother is attached; the teacher is attached—yet detached. At the end of the school day, the child goes home to his/her own mother; and the teacher, if she is a mother, returns to her own child.

Most certainly, there are sound reasons why a teacher should avoid applying a mothering discourse at work.⁶³ For one, it is good sense to maintain a clear distinction between the public and private in education. Teachers should not be attempting to raise students in their own image. Moreover, teachers who believe that they are helping their students by becoming a mother-substitute may actually be doing more harm than good. Studies have shown that these teachers tend to act out of "deficit thinking". They believe that their students are lacking in some way at home and hence, require the teacher to meet those needs in response. Unfortunately, the teacher's assessment may be based on personal experiences; whether they had been (or wished they had been) cared for in that way themselves.⁶⁴ Taken to an extreme, this kind of thinking can cloud judgement and careful listening, or worse, be mistaken for arrogance or disrespect of the child's family and their (cultural) ways of doing, living, and being.

Sometimes, it may even expose the teacher to excessive responsibility for the child's life or future.[65]

In addition, there are broader, macro-systemic reasons why teaching should never be confused with mothering. A woman, for example, should never be stopped from entering the teaching profession simply because she is not a mother. Similarly, a man should not avoid entering the teaching profession because he could never be a mother. It needs to be emphasised that early childhood educators need not be parents to fully understand their role.[66] Some of the best teachers I hired at Wee Care were men, non-parents, or both! But the feminisation of teaching is real, and it has been an impediment to some men wanting to be early years' teachers. These men find themselves facing excessive suspicion, even though their motivations to teach young children are genuine and well-intentioned.[67]

Early childhood education in Singapore and around the world would benefit from having more men as teachers. Research has shown that male teachers are better able to distinguish whether a boy's unruly play is typical behaviour or unacceptable aggression. Without the inputs that male teachers (and fathers) bring to school—including preschool!—masculinity in boys is often misconstrued and interpreted as negative, undesirable.[68]

Disequilibrium in the gender workforce in early childhood is made all the more unfortunate by research that demonstrates that both men and women equally believe in the importance of caring in teaching. In fact, both genders ascribe to a concept of caring that is **ethical**. It is a part of the teacher's **professional** identity.[69]

Indeed, there are perils associated with accepting teaching as mothers' work. It may serve to devalue the profession considerably.[70] Moreover, if teaching is viewed as a "natural" component of women's labour, it may present the false impression that women do not need monetary rewards or public recognition in return for such work.[71] One response to this kind of patriarchal subjugation was the decision in the early decades of the 20th century to base early childhood practices on the science of developmental psychology.[72] By aligning their field in this way, teachers effectively sought to distance their work from any association with home and maternal practices. They wanted to promote an image of themselves as skilled, specialised, and authoritative.[73]

But can love and professionalism not co-exist?

On the one hand, there are benefits to cultivating a school ethos that is loving and caring. A school environment that is emotionally intelligent produces children who are emotionally intelligent themselves. Teachers who are deeply and personally involved with children have also reported higher levels of fulfilment at work.[74] More significant, perhaps, is the knowledge that when we teach with love, we have the potential of influencing the child's life beyond his/her time in our classroom and hence, the families they represent and society too. It has been observed that students who have experienced the care of a teacher are more likely to develop good self-esteem and the trust necessary to take risks and reach higher levels of academic achievement.[75]

On the other hand, the emotional distance afforded by an objective and rational approach to teaching and its challenges is valuable and indeed, in some contexts, necessary. How else could a teacher evaluate a bullying incident dispassionately and respond accordingly? Or—and this has happened at least once or twice in my career—adjudicate between two warring students, one of whom in a fit of anger has bitten the other child? Love—by its nature, one-sided and prejudicial—may not always be able to inhibit its desire to shield the perpetrator. For teachers, loving every child (both the one in the wrong and the one who is right) and yet being true to one's professional identity simultaneously can be a complex undertaking filled with tensions, anxieties, and contradictions.

But love matters.

It was not an accident that Wee Care was called what it was; "wee" being the informal Scottish word for "little", and "care", its demonstrative anchor; my considered hope and resolve that the school would be a place where little people would be loved and cared for unreservedly, without embarrassment or apology.

I can still recall many moments over my 21 years at the school, especially during staff meetings, when I would affirm the importance of being professional and yet loving and caring. It was like a repeated slogan, to be honest, one that found its way into our mission and vision statements, as well as our staff handbook and yearly performance appraisal forms.

We should ensure that our uniforms are ironed.

We should not shout at the children.

We should keep our classrooms neat and tidy.

We should never, ever, discipline any child physically.

We should smile and be welcoming.

> *We should never, ever, change a child out of wet clothing, or even a soiled diaper, in view of other children or parents.*
>
> *We should ensure that we are always ready for our lessons—learning materials, equipment, props, and books, all prepared and within reach, in good time.*
>
> *We should not neglect the children with special needs, the parents with extra requests, that painful additional mile.*
>
> *We should place the tables this way; no, that way, so that everyone can see the board.*
>
> *We should not place the chairs like that; a child may trip and fall.*

Was this effort to care and yet maintain a deliberate professionalism in our daily practices, year after year, exhausting, wearying? Most certainly.

Was it rewarding? Oh, yes.

But did loving the children also lead to many bittersweet moments; those graduation days of saying goodbye, in particular, when we were happy at the milestones reached but sad too that there would only be mere photographs and memories left of our days together? Quite definitely.

I also learnt—too late perhaps—that fostering a culture of love at school meant caring for our staff and their needs too. Care in this case included the teachers' aspirations and opinions. It included tangible expressions of concern towards their own children and families at times. We did what we could where and when we could, extending significant fee subsidies to the offspring of staff members, adhering to statutory requirements for maternity and childcare leave and further, rewarding extra days of bonus leave at the end of every school year so that everyone could get a good, long break to spend with significant others and loved ones as needed.

And very often, most of the time in fact, the love we extended to each other and to our students and their families was fully reciprocated. Mutuality was achieved, in other words[76]—that state of relationship that is so persuasively ephemeral, yet so real.

> I'll tie the flowers to my hair,
>   the chocolates to my tum,
> wrap the cards around the hugs of
> oranges and mooncakes you sent me via that
> spaceship we sent off yesterday—where,
> somewhere in Toyland,
> I ate the pie and the salad,
> looked at your pictures, and read without one tear
> the letters you had scrawled in large hand
> across the white of that paper sky.

Are such objects or words manifestations of love and care, just as changing a diaper a duty filled with tenderness and concern? To me, any form of care I show is the outward expression of a love I feel inside. It has been described that in a caring encounter, the one who is caring meets the person being cared for with "engrossment", that is, with full attention and openness to the other person's perspective and situation. In addition, the encounter must feature "motivational displacement"—the willingness to give priority, even if only briefly, to the aims and needs of the one being cared for.[77]

Of course, there are different forms of caring and what may be regarded as caring by one teacher may be exemplified quite differently by another teacher. Interestingly, when teachers are asked about this, caring as "commitment to teaching" tends to feature quite prominently as the indicator by which teachers themselves identify "real teachers" from the ones who are perceived as not taking their job seriously.[78]

There were, of course, teachers who came to Wee Care who did not or could not, for whatever reason—and perhaps for very good reasons—align with our caring ethos wholeheartedly. I do not think that they were not suitable for teaching—most certainly not—but I do hope that they succeeded eventually in securing what they were looking for. In fact, I hope many of them stayed in the field and were not turned away by the intensity of the dedication that was being asked of them.

The bottom line, in effect, was that I could not, on the basis of the values I wanted the company to uphold, settle on a less caring or less loving school. Furthermore, I had already reckoned—for myself anyway—that a woman's capacity to care is a strength, not a weakness. A mother's capacity to love, forceful, uncompromising. When a teacher/mother brings her shared experiences and knowledge to school, she brings a dimension of heart and soul to her teaching that may not be found in the same way elsewhere. We should stop making apologies for teaching that incorporates the positives of mothering, caring, and loving, while being conscious at the same time of the potential pitfalls and tensions that such a complex role will invariably entail. But most of all, we should keep in mind that universally, good teachers are identified as those who care.[79]

They look different now, the children whom I taught and cared for in their early years. I would probably not recognise many of them if I chanced to pass them on the street, and they would probably not remember me either. But I cherish the memories I have of them, and of the love we shared at school.

> *John, who cried and cried when he first started school, and whom I cuddled and prayed for in the pantry, that he would stop wailing and enjoy being with his friends and teachers.*
>
> *Yu Fatt, whose hand I had to hold while he endured stitches after jumping excitedly in the playground, losing his balance and falling.*
> *Thomas, whom I had to accompany to the Emergency Room too, and Matthew, another boy, with another ER story. The exuberance of these boys for all that life was making available to them became the frame for the heart that rose and fell through the pain of their ordeals.*

Keith, Joel, Ginette and more, who snuggled up to me on the airbed when we pretended to have a slumber party—pyjamas and all—in Language Arts.

Iris, who drew me a picture of a butterfly and wrote, "Thank you for teaching me" next to it. She will never know how I had struggled to find the time that day to substitute her sick teacher.

And Karen, who would smile, laugh, and jump up and down whenever she saw me at the start of the school day.

To each of you,

With my love,
Teacher Denise xx

---

55 Goldstein, L. S. (1998). *Teaching with love: A feminist approach to early childhood education.* New York: Peter Lang.
56 Kohl, H. R. (1984). *Growing minds: On becoming a teacher.* New York: Harper & Row.
57 West, C. (1996). Democracy's promise, democracy's peril. *ASCD Education Update, 38*(3). http://www.ascd.org/publications/newsletters/education-update/may96/vol38/num03/Democracy's-Promise,-Democracy's-Peril.aspx
58 Ayers, W. (1989). *The good preschool teacher: Six teachers reflect on their lives.* New York: Teachers College Press.
59 Matthew 19:14, Mark 10:14, Luke 18:16. *The Holy Bible* (NIV version).
60 Lightfoot, S. L. (1977). Family-school interactions: The cultural image of mothers and teachers. *Signs: Journal of Women in Culture and Society, 3*(2), 395–408.
61 Aspinwall, K., & Drummond, M. J. (1989). Socialized into primary teaching. In H. De Lyon, & F. W. Migniuolo (Eds.), *Women teachers: Issues and experiences* (pp. 11–22). Milton Keynes: Open University Press.

62 Katz, L. G. (1980). Mothering and teaching: Some significant distinctions. In L. G. Katz (Ed.), *Current topics in early childhood education Vol. III* (pp. 47–63). Norwood, NJ: Ablex Publishing.
63 James, J. H. (2012). Caring for "others": Examining the interplay of mothering and deficit discourses in teaching. *Teacher and Teacher Education, 28*(2), 165–173.
64 For example, see McBride, N., & Grieshaber, S. (2001). Professional caring as mothering. In S. Reifel, & M. H. Brown (Eds.), *Early education and care, and reconceptualizing play* (pp. 169–202). Bingley, UK: Emerald Publishing Ltd. See also, Goldstein, K., Goldstein, L. S., & Lake, V. E. (2003). The impact of field experience on preservice teachers' understandings of caring. *Teacher Education Quarterly, 30*(3), 115–132.
65 James, J. H. (2010). Teachers as mothers in the elementary classroom: Negotiating the needs of self and other. *Gender and Education, 22*(5), 521–534.
66 James, J. H. (2012). Caring for "others": Examining the interplay of mothering and deficit discourses in teaching. *Teaching and Teacher Education, 28*(2), 165–173.
67 Skelton, C. (1994) Sex, male teachers and young children. *Gender and Education, 6*(1), 87–93.
68 For more information about men in early childhood education, please read Jensen, J. (1998). Men as workers in childcare services. In C. Owen, C. Cameron, & P. Moss (Eds.), *Men as workers in services for young children: Issues of mixed gender workforce*. London: Institute of Education. See also Tavecchio, L. (2003). Presentation at the "Men in Childcare" conference, Belfry, Ghent, November 28. 2003; and Peeters, J. (2007). Including men in early childhood education: Insights from the European experience. *NZ Research in Early Childhood Education, 10,* 15–24.
69 Vogt, F. (2002). A caring teacher: Explorations into primary school teachers' professional identity and ethic of care. *Gender and Education, 14*(3), 251–264.
70 Grumet, M. R. (1988). *Bitter milk: Women and teaching*. Amherst, MA: The University of Massachusetts Press.
71 Acker, S. (1999). *The realities of teachers' work: Never a dull moment*. London: Cassell.
72 Goldstein, L. S. (1993, October). *The distance between feminism and early childhood education: An historical perspective*. [Paper presentation]. Reconceptualising Early Childhood Education: Theory, Research and Practice Conference, Ann Arbor, MI, United States.
73 Bloch, M. N. (1987). Becoming scientific and professional: An historical perspective on the aims and effects of early education. In T. S. Popkewitz (Ed.), *The formation of school subjects* (pp. 25–62). New York: The Falmer Press.
74 Nias, J. (1989). *Primary teachers talking: A study of teaching as work*. London: Routledge.
75 Goldstein, K., Goldstein, L. S., & Lake, V. E. (2003). The impact of field experience on preservice teachers' understandings of caring. *Teacher Education Quarterly, 30*(3), 115–132. See also, Helm, C. (2007). Teacher dispositions affecting self-esteem and student performance. *The Clearing House: A Journal of Educational Strategies, Issues and Ideas, 80*(3), 109–110.
76 Noddings, N. (1984). *Caring: A Feminine Approach to Ethics & Moral Education*. Berkeley, CA: University of California Press.
77 Noddings, N. (1984). *Caring: A Feminine Approach to Ethics & Moral Education*. Berkeley, CA: University of California Press.
78 Nias, J. (1989). *Primary teachers talking: A study of teaching as work*. London: Routledge.
79 For example, see Noddings, N. (1992). *The challenge to care in schools: An alternative approach to education*. New York, NY: Teachers College Press; and Ashley, M., & Lee, J. (2003) *Women teaching boys: Caring and working in the primary school*. Stoke on Trent, UK: Trentham Books.

PLAYING ALL THE TIME

All children play; although the exact form and frequency of the play will depend on an assortment of factors. These would include the age and gender of the child, the cultural milieu that the child is in, as well as the precise social setting (which itself incorporates the physical environment that the child is playing in, the peers who are present, and even the adults who are participating).

On this last point, I have noticed that not all adults are able to play with young children. It is almost as if these adults have forgotten how to play, although they will be playing their own grown-up sports and/or games e.g. tennis, basketball, billiards, bubble soccer, laser tag, and the like! My own mother has taken a liking to Rummikub, the tile-based board game that combines elements of gin rummy and mah-jong.

No, what I am referring to is the ability of the adult to play with the child in a way that the little one understands and is captivated. You may ask why this is important. Well, studies have shown that adult availability and co-engagement in play can extend the duration and complexity of a child's play.[80] By inference, adults playing with children can broaden the latters' cognitive, language, and socio-emotional skills because play on its own is a powerful enhancer of these abilities.[81]

Now, if you are a parent reading this, please do not think that I am trying to make you feel guilty for not spending more time with your child or for needing a break from your child at times. The stress of work and other life pressures can critically undermine our capacity to play **like** a child and **with** a child. After all, play requires a certain kind of psychological state; one needs to be relaxed and happy in order to play freely and imaginatively without inhibition. My own babies were a handful. When they were growing up, my head would whirl with their incessant chatter and demands for attention—especially when they were bored!—their persistent requests for something or another—a book or toy now, TV or the playground later.

"*Kepala pusing*," my grandmother would complain, "*mak nenek!*"* Yet it truly is a privilege to have a child to play with. Now that my children are all grown up and doing their own thing—out with friends or in internet land—I miss having someone to play with. Life is not the same.

This rumination, however, only serves to underscore what I think was an implicit goal at Wee Care throughout its pioneering years. The school was not just about us, the teachers and the children, engaging and learning together. It was also about what we could do as teachers to build families up. It was about our role in enhancing the bonds of relationship between us all. In other words, the reciprocal

---

* My Peranakan grandmother would use these terms of endearment frequently. *Kepala pusing* literally means "head going around and around" (or "headache") and *mak nenek* (directly translated, as "mother-grandmother") means "a double nag".

relationships between the children and their parents were just as important to me as the relationships we had with the children and their parents.

At the risk of belabouring this point, I used to display the diagram below in our employee handbook to explain the back-and-forth of relationships at Wee Care, not just in terms of communication and interaction, but also in the emotional impact one party might potentially have on another. Applied specifically to play, the diagram was used to express both the coherence and the principle that parent-child play at the preschool should be mutually enriching.

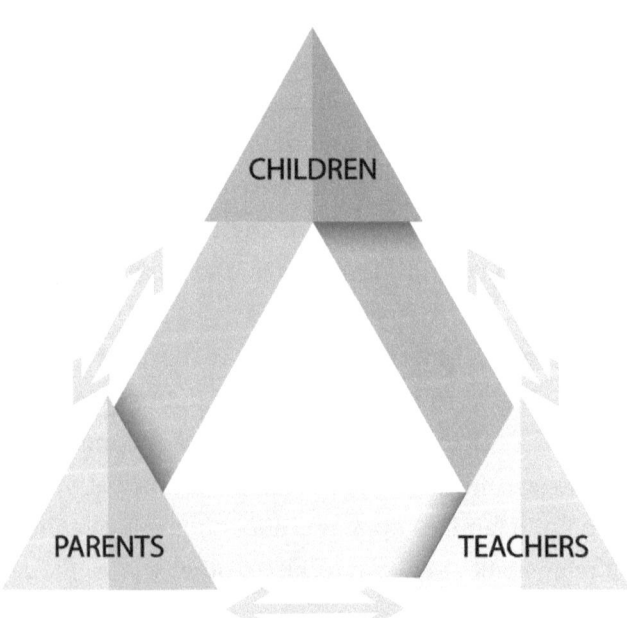

Also, that we could positively and tangibly engage with the parents as collaborators—and conspirators!—during play. Thus, if you had been a parent at Wee Care at the time, you might have been asked to be an imaginary shark under the parachute, or the one holding the bucket that the children would aim balls into (or alternately, throwing the balls that the children would catch). In the infant playgroup sessions, you might have bounced your baby on an inflatable car or encouraged object permanence by shaking a rattle, hiding it under a scarf before shaking the same rattle under the scarf. These activities were all very powerful in my view, in cementing the frame of relational ties that true and effective learning hinges on.

Many years later, a professor at the National Institute of Education (or NIE, where I did the first part of my doctorate) told me that this diagram expressed a postmodern ideal. By this, he probably meant that relationships conceived as a meeting between equals must assume a position of relativism and subjectivity.[82] There is no "truth", as it were, because truth is a matter of a person's worldview, which can be shaped by many things. Many philosophers now would criticise this assertion to be hypocritical and **untrue** since the statement itself purports to be true (there are limitations in other words, in how far we can take postmodern beliefs). Nonetheless, the aspiration that we had at Wee Care to foster deep, reciprocal, and positive relationships (not just the aim of teaching young children) was a sincere and heartfelt desire. The warmth and kindness that we sought to nurture in our environment was one of the main factors, I believe, distinguishing us from other settings.

And so, from this vantage point, we spent each day at Wee Care talking, playing, and making friends. Play made the days go by quickly. Play infused all of our lessons. It was the medium by which learning took place as well as the goal, and what a goal, if you think about it, to just play!

Interestingly, I remember more fathers than mothers playing with their children at Wee Care. This was probably a function of the simple fact that many of the dads who attended our Saturday morning parent-toddler playgroup classes were taking the opportunity to spend time with their little ones after a long week at work. Mothers, too, may have jumped at the chance to get some downtime or me time while both the baby and husband were out. At the same time, I would like to think that the fathers were willing to attend our playgroup sessions because they enjoyed the play themselves. We did strive to make every playgroup session fun and organised, with lots of interesting and novel activities to engage in each week. In addition, I hope the dads felt that they could attend because there were no stressful expectations or hidden agendas of any sort to be a "good" or "perfect" father during the lessons. They really were just ideal occasions to spend quality time with one's child. On our part, we never once misunderstood our role as a service provider; as teachers, we always aimed to be on hand to answer questions, support the experience, and enhance the children's play and learning.

Having said this, it does take a measure of skill and patience to play with a child and I think all forward-looking parents learn to do this with aplomb over time. In addition, practice probably compels a parent to learn—quite rapidly—to play with a measure of wisdom and caution too. Once, a father at Wee Care threw his toddler son so high in the air during a group game that he almost missed catching the boy as he came down. Thankfully, these near-accidents were rare. By and large, Wee Care fathers were a positive influence in every playgroup session. They would "chew" their way dutifully through imaginary cakes and pizzas; strum or blow into toy musical instruments; lift, swing, and dance with their children and/or change diapers like pros! Once in a while though—and these incidents would really touch me— we would have an exhausted father crawl into class and fall asleep on the floor after a protracted red-eye flight (some from as far as London or New York). Such was the extent of these fathers' dedication and sacrifice.

What do you remember playing as a child? How did you play?

I remember ...

> *my father and mother teaching me to make sandcastles at the beach—how we would pour seawater into a dug-up moat and press tiny seashells into the fragile towers;*
>
> *running about my grandparents' home, playing some variation of Wolf, trying to catch my brother and male cousin who were faster sprinters than me;*
>
> *cycling, embarrassed that I still needed training wheels;*
>
> *playing with the dog; walking with my grandfather in the evenings around the estate, afraid of other dogs who seemed so large and ferocious;*
>
> *befriending the neighbourhood children who lived in the same Toa Payoh block of flats, going up and down the stairs or ancient machines we called lifts,*

cuddling the stray kittens and feeding them drops of milk that our Indian friends had surreptitiously sneaked out of their mother's kitchen, then

swinging as high as I could go at the playground, before

running to the provision shop for coloured ice pops

~ quite oblivious of the time ~

then hearing Auntie, who lived across from us on the sixth floor, screaming through her open window for Ah Pang, my playmate, to come home soon or she would cane her till she died ...

being Princess Leia in a dark room with my maternal cousins, watching the boys scream and shout as they shot invisible rays at each other; huddling next to Luke Skywalker against Darth Vader who had set up camp along the other end of the bed frame, knowing that I would not be taken because I could always run out of the room and state emphatically, "I'm not playing anymore!"

hurdling "zero point" with my friends in school, so proud of being able to fly that high, getting over that rubber-band rope without falling or stumbling.

Play was a big part of my childhood and I wanted it to be a part of every child's journey at Wee Care too.

It was thus a tremendous let-down when I learnt that many parents did not feel the same way about the importance of play in preschool, an issue that I will explore in greater detail in the next chapter. I was also taken by surprise when parents surfaced protectionist perspectives about play that I could not have anticipated simply because their attitudes arose from historical and cultural contexts that were fundamentally different from the one I had grown up in.

By this, I am not referring to dilemmas related to sharing or not sharing, or being included or excluded from play—although these issues did lead to minor flare-ups once in a while. Sometime in the mid-2010s, for instance, a mother, so incensed that her daughter was crying from not having been invited to a fellow classmate's birthday party, called and shouted at me over the phone about how I could have permitted such unfairness to take place at Wee Care. Of course, I had not even been aware that the birthday girl had been giving out party invitation cards to selected members of her class. Thankfully, a quick call to the birthday girl's mother put the matter to rest. An extra invitation was extended—very graciously—and the party proceeded as planned without any further hiccups. In incidents such as these or when the children did not want to share toys or space, we took the opportunity to empathise and to understand, and to teach or cultivate social skills and emotional intelligence along the way. We adults probably learnt as much as the children did at these times.

Even behaviour problems occurring during play were easier to tackle than the dilemmas brought about by worldview differences. A child biting another in the heat of a disagreement in the playground or playroom would always be just and sufficient cause for the teacher to intervene. In early childhood education, **every** child is assured psychological safety, intellectual safety, and physical health and safety.[83] After a biting episode, both the victim and biter would be "restored" so to speak, using a social-emotional approach that focused on self-awareness, other-awareness, forgiveness (and also, saying "sorry" and asking to be forgiven) as well as concrete strategies (such as social stories or self-control techniques) to prevent any chance of repeated aggression in the future. In more persistent cases, it was sometimes necessary for me to suspend the biter from class for a few days. But these instances were relatively uncommon. With coaching and the use of rewards and reminders, most parents were able to address their child's negative behaviour(s) quickly and successfully.

No, the main dilemma that I still think about is the one involving imaginary play with replica guns, knives, and/or swords; but primarily guns. In Wee Care's early years, we would create pretend-play scenarios in the Open Learning playroom around the themes of "jungle exploration", "the army", or "the police". Quite ignorant at the time of how some mothers perceived toy weapons, we would provide our little explorers, soldiers, and/or police officers with flimsy plastic pistols, the kind that you could purchase quite easily from any provision shop in old Singapore or even Toys 'R' Us. During play times, and in complete innocence, we would enact scenarios where the children would shoot at imaginary predators in the jungle to protect themselves. Or, they would be prompted to chase and catch us, the teacher-criminals, and put us in jail. To me at the time, these were all part of the socio-cognitive enculturation that must take place for children to "learn to think and behave in ways that reflect their community's culture".[84]

"Ugh," the mother said and shuddered, "why do you have guns in here?"
"It's just pretend."
"Ugh, no."

I tried to say that Singaporean boys would enlist in National Service eventually, and that research had, in fact, shown evidence for a "cathartic" theory in play. According to this theory, play with imaginary weapons can help children release aggressive feelings and reduce the likelihood of aggressive behaviours outside of play.[85] In fact, some play therapy researchers and practitioners have gone so far as to argue that young children need "acting-out-aggressive-release" play opportunities so that they can let go of aggressive tensions and tendencies.[86] Specifically, one case study has shown that banning play with gun themes does not eliminate young children's interest in weapons. Rather, it causes children to hide their play from their teachers, which can result in a higher risk of unsupervised aggression.[87] In contrast, teachers responding to children's play intentions constructively can turn imaginary acts of aggression into fruitful learning experiences.[88] Indeed, and paradoxically, when preschoolers who engage in pretend gun play are interviewed about it, they respond in a way that demonstrates an increased understanding of social justice and the need to control violence, especially with the use of problem-solving strategies.[89]

Unfortunately, the mother was not convinced and our conversation ended on an unsatisfactory, incomplete note. Later, I shared her concerns with one of my trusted teachers, a kind and mature lady from New Zealand whose opinion I respected considerably.

"My son never watched any television growing up," she replied thoughtfully, "but one day, while walking home, he picked up a small stick from a tree, and used it like a gun to shoot at imaginary targets."

Jeannie's experience as a mother confirmed the findings I had read about in research. But I still felt unsettled because I genuinely wanted to address the mother's concerns. From what I had managed to piece together, she was from a cultural milieu where apprehensions about gun violence were quite understandable and completely valid.

About a year or so later, a new family signed up at Wee Care and concerns about aggression arose again, although from a slightly different angle. At that week's playgroup session, I read an abridged version of *Saint George and the Dragon*. In case you have not read this legend yourself, it is a classic tale of a hero slaying an evil dragon that has been terrorising people. I could tell while reading the book that the new mother was not happy. Her face showed a great deal of discomfort but I was not sure, at the time, the exact cause of the uneasiness. It did not take long for me to find out. Once there was a quiet moment, she asked me why I had selected a book that glorified violence against animals. She said that she was a vegetarian and did not want her children hearing stories about animals—even mythical ones—being killed (even though the children were not vegetarian themselves).

This time, I was silent. In both incidents, I knew that the mothers had noble intentions for feeling and speaking the way they did. But I was nonplussed because acceding to their requests would prevent the rest of the school population from enjoying tales about good and evil, heroes and heroines. It would also constrain the children's freedom to play and learn important constructs related to morality and ethics.

Eventually though, it was large-scale global events outside of our tiny world at Wee Care that helped me reach a resolution. The extinction of many animal species and the environmental crises besetting our times, the events of 9/11 and other terrorist attacks (some very close to Singapore), raised a collective consciousness and sensitivity that I was not immune to myself. Slowly and progressively, all forms of imaginary gun-play (including play with pretend swords and spears) were gradually phased out of Wee Care. Our culture changed with the world and with it, our children's ways of learning right and wrong.

The rise of the internet contributed to this shift obviously, what with the visceral power of appalling images and/or stories conveyed so immediately and emotionally through it. But at least we can be assured that the generations to come will not necessarily need pretend-play scenarios to process and work through innate drives related to power and combat. Indeed, with the ubiquitous availability of gaming applications these days, the same need for "acting-out-aggressive-release" play opportunities may be found through newer modalities in cyberspace.

However, only time will tell if play during the early childhood years has lost something in the creation of new narratives in this flat world.[90]

> Will we just fish, or is that hunting
> and hurting still our world
> where cops and robbers
> and dress-up games
> go belly-up with the whales we bounced on
> and wished alive?

I hope the predicament is apparent. There is a fine line between protecting our children's hearts and minds and controlling their play so that they miss learning important things. But we also know that the nexus between the broader culture and the events that take place at home or in a classroom is populated by well-meaning teachers and parents who often and invariably find themselves in the powerful position[91] of having to make difficult decisions on behalf of their students/children. This challenge is exacerbated by the realisation that one day, our children will be the ones making the decisions.

But until that day arrives, I guess, we can only play on ... just very carefully.

---

80   For example, see Bateman, A. (2015). *Conversation analysis and early childhood education: The co-production of knowledge and relationships*. Surrey, UK: Ashgate Publishing Ltd. See also Kalliala, M. (2014). Toddlers as both more and less competent social actors in Finnish day care centres. *Early Years, 34*(1), 4–17; and Jung, J. (2013). Teachers' roles in infants' play and its changing nature in a dynamic group care context. *Early Childhood Research Quarterly, 28*(1), 187–198.
81   Barnett, L. A. (1990). Developmental benefits of play for children. *Journal of Leisure Research, 22*(2), 138–153.
82   For a brief explanation on postmodernism, please see: Duignan, B. (2020, September 4). Postmodernism. In *Encyclopedia Britannica*. www.britannica.com/topic/postmodernism-philosophy
83   Velu, G., & Loh, H. M. (2010). *Code of ethics handbook: An essential companion for daily practice*. Singapore: Association for Early Childhood Educators (Singapore).
84   Berk, L. E., & Winsler, A. (1995). *Scaffolding children's learning: Vygotsky and early childhood education (NAEYC Research into Practice Series: Volume 7)*. Washington, D.C.: National Association for the Education of Young Children (NAEYC).
85   Laue, C. E. (2015). *Toy guns in play therapy: Controversy and current practice* [Unpublished doctoral dissertation]. The Chicago School of Professional Psychology.
86   Landreth, G. L. (2012). *Play therapy: The art of the relationship*. New York, NY: Routledge.
87   Delaney, K. K. (2017). Playing at violence: Lock-down drills, "bad guys" and the construction of "acceptable" play in early childhood. *Early Child Development and Care, 187*(5–6), 878–895.
88   Logue, M. E. & Detour, A. (2011). "You be the bad guy": A new role for teachers in supporting children's dramatic play. *Early Childhood Research & Practice, 13*(1), 1–14.

89 Bauman, J. (2015). Examining how and why children in my transitional kindergarten classroom engage in pretend gunplay. *Studying Teacher Education*, *11*(2), 191–210.
90 Friedman, T. L. (2005). *The world is flat: A brief history of the twenty-first century*. New York: Farrar, Straus and Giroux.
91 Freeman, N. K. & Brown, M. H. (2004). The moral and ethical dimensions of controlling play. In R. L. Clements & L. Fiorentino (Eds.), *The child's right to play: A global approach* (pp. 9–21). Westport, CT: Praeger Publishers.

7

SURVIVING THE COMPETITION

One of the first books I read as a new mother was *How to Have a Smarter Baby*.[92] I was still in Hong Kong at the time. An acquaintance, who was also expecting a baby, looked at me aghast when she caught sight of the book in my hands.

"Really?" she bleated politely.

I was surprised. Did not every mother want her baby to thrive?

Her response, however, had given me a sneak peek into the world of competitive parenting. In this world, particularly in places like Singapore and Hong Kong, all parents are training their children to race to the top. In the process, you must urge other parents not to be excessive while simultaneously appearing to be as far removed from being a tiger parent[93] yourself.

Cynicism aside, there are parents who thoroughly enjoy the cut and thrust of spirited contest and who will live this out vicariously through their children. But most parents (I think) dislike the hypercompetitive environment that they themselves were raised in (or recognise its flaws and pitfalls, at least). It is an environment that they probably still inhabit at their respective workplaces. If they could, many of these parents would probably prefer having their children grow up on gentler and kinder terms.

Or maybe I am simply describing my own idealised perspective. I had not had a child to win. I had conceived a child to love and nurture. This child-centred perspective—this belief in the value of **every child**—was at the heart of the ethos I sought to cultivate at Wee Care.

Unfortunately, cultural context can mean and determine everything. Or in my case, undermine the best of intentions.

In the 1990s, Singapore was still fixated on meritocracy as a "core principle of governance ... as close as anything gets to being a national ideology".[94] In its local form, merit is conceived of as a combination of effort and talent, both inherent and cultivated. Meritocracy is a "practice that rewards individual merit with social rank, job positions, higher incomes or general recognition and prestige".[95]

In 1997, the year I started Wee Care, then Prime Minister Goh Chok Tong introduced a catchphrase to further articulate and extend Singapore's meritocratic vision for education. The axiom was "Thinking Schools, Learning Nation" (TSLN) and its aim was to "prepare children for the future and to prepare them to be continually prepared for the future".[96] It generated initiatives such as Ability-Driven Education (or ADE), a paradigm in which success is achievable by anyone in possession of the talent and willingness to work hard. The ADE affirmed the principle of meritocracy; that social mobility is the outcome of one's effort rather than one's social, political, economic, or cultural background.[97]

A complete discussion about the advantages and disadvantages of meritocracy is far beyond the scope of this book, but you can imagine,

I think, how a performance-focused education system aligned awkwardly with my conviction that children should be valued for **who they are** and not what they can achieve necessarily. It also sat badly with my concern that atypical children should not be penalised for needing different definitions of success. In practice, what this meant, in effect, was that many Singaporean parents at the time of Wee Care's founding did not always subscribe to my enthusiasm for "learning through play"; not unless a clear link could be demonstrated between this pedagogical approach and future academic—and by deduction, employment and economic—gains.

For many years, thus, I had to bear the constant discouragement of being told that Wee Care was simply not academic enough; that while it was all good and fine that the children could play and have fun in preschool, surely they would need a thorough grounding in Maths and Mandarin and reading and writing too, in preparation for primary school? I found myself on the defensive a lot during those early years. I had to explain our specific teaching methodology again and again; why it was better, how it compared with the Montessori or flashcards approach, and how certain I was that children who attended Wee Care would not lose out in some way.

Quite understandably, most people assumed (and may still assume) that "play" is just messing about and in a way, this definition is correct. In early childhood education, play is an end in itself. It is not a means to an end, which is what most parents want play to be. Parents want to be assured that whatever the play activity the child is engaged in, especially at school, it is supporting the child's acquisition of an important skill like talking or reading or counting or making friends. Like most parents, I have understood these sentiments and **used** play in this same (instrumental) way as both a teacher and a parent.

Play must meet learning goals.

True or False?

To the more fervent advocates and proponents of play, true "child's play"[98] is process-oriented rather than product-oriented. It is also creative, flexible, spontaneous and where possible, imaginative. In **real** play, the child has the autonomy to change the goals and rules of play as he/she likes. The wonderful consequence of this would be the child's ongoing engagement and intrinsic motivation for the activity. Interestingly, play can be paradoxical too: fun but frustrating. Have you ever tried building a tent with a blanket draped over chairs but the blanket keeps slipping off?

Let's be firefighters today!
No, no, no, I want to cook ... I want to cook pasta for Mummy.

You be the baby.
No! You be the baby. I am a princess.
Okay, you be the princess. I will cook, okay? Teacher Denise, look, I made chicken.

Educationalists who support learning through play tend to agree with the famous psychologist Jean Piaget that play—genuine play, not enforced play (as if such a thing could really exist)—is the vehicle for children's construction of knowledge. To Piaget, who documented his observations in the first half of the 20th century, play offers children the experiences necessary to construct three basic kinds of knowledge: physical knowledge, logical-mathematical knowledge, and even social knowledge, but in the reverse direction. Children apply the ideas that they have learnt in social situations (like social roles and social rules) to their play. Gradually, through rich and repeated play experiences, the child's mind develops: abstract thought increases and egocentric thinking declines.[99]

These days, early childhood practitioners all over the world recognise the value of play (and tangible, play-full experiences) and seek to use it as the "medium of instruction" (almost like a language) in their classrooms.

Let's count the oranges.

Yes, you're right, the letter O looks like an orange.

Can oranges roll? Why is that so?

Who likes marmalade? Shall we give it a try?

That's right, you can poke cloves into oranges to make a nice-smelling pomander.

In the 1990s in Singapore, unfortunately, academic outcomes still mattered more than the mere construction of knowledge. Even though my teachers and I spent an inordinate amount of time each week preparing our classrooms for all kinds of sensory, imaginative, messy, conceptual, or social kinds of play, it was an uphill battle convincing many parents to invest in this pedagogical approach.

This is not to say that we did not have our supporters. There were Singaporean parents who understood and wanted the kind of teaching we were providing, although they were not as many as I would have liked. Our approach was also very much welcomed by expatriate families who had struggled to find a setting in Singapore with a small child-to-teacher ratio that was authentically play- and experience-based. Some of these expatriate mothers became our biggest fans, contributing their time and effort to support our activities voluntarily, such as driving children to and from field trip locations, and even coming by during a term break once to whitewash our walls. I will always remember and be forever grateful to these parents, both local and expatriate, of those pioneering years.

Ironically, nestled between these groups of clients was a small subset of local parents who wanted their children to experience **both** the play-based learning we were providing and the academic drilling available in other local preschools. In fact, one mother told me that when her daughter got to the right age, she would attend Wee Care in the morning ("for the play and social development") and a PCF kindergarten* in the afternoon! At the time, PCF kindergartens were known to be academically rigorous with lots of writing worksheets to complete each day, as well as spelling quizzes and Mandarin dictation tests to surmount each week.

> Like tentacles winding—we groan,
> grasp, grapple, and gasp simply
> for our children
> to be alive
> and happy
> and free.

---

* PCF Kindergartens were run by the PAP Community Foundation, the charitable arm of the People's Action Party. They are now called PCF Sparkletots.

> But *kiasu*** is the cake that
> invites the hands that slice it.

It was hugely disconcerting to me that a hypercompetitive mindset had infiltrated the early childhood years. It kept me so perplexed that I eventually studied the phenomenon and wrote about it in my doctoral dissertation.[100] The research I conducted revealed that in Singapore, deep-seated beliefs about meritocracy and pragmatism go hand-in-hand with neoliberal tenets of competition and a self-regulating free market to justify academic acceleration.

What does this mean in less gobbledygook? Well, the parents I interviewed said that for Singapore to "survive", we have to acknowledge and reward the best people (students, workers, etc.) even if it means training their children from young to be resilient. Resilience, in this case, would be to bear hardship, overcome challenges, and demonstrate discipline and/or the right attitude in school and one's lessons. Thus cultivated, the child would be better prepared and poised to reap benefits, bonuses, and advantages in the form of good jobs and longer-term employment prospects. He/She would be better able to compete successfully for a tangible slice of the economic pie. Indeed, in Singapore, a market of the "self" exists where one has fewer or more, better or worse academic and/or professional qualifications.

Interestingly, the parents I spoke to in my research referred to meritocracy in a variety of ways. Sometimes, it meant keeping up with one's peers or getting ready for primary school. At other times, it was

---

** *Kiasu* is a term derived from the Hokkien Chinese vernacular. It means to fear losing (怕输) and is commonly used in Singapore to refer to anxious, greedy, or selfish behaviours.

about competing to get into the best secondary schools. Meritocracy was so deeply imbued as a set of taken-for-granted assumptions that parents did not mind material incentives like candy or toys being used to motivate their children in tuition or enrichment lessons. At the same time, there were notable omissions. Most of the parents did not talk about their children leading **purposeful** lives or engaging in activities that were creative, adventurous, or developmentally appropriate.

My research was conducted between 2012 and 2014. I would like to think that things have changed (improved?) since. But I cannot be sure. The interviews had also revealed that in Singapore, "governmentality"[101] exists. This concept, first conceived by the French philosopher and social theorist, Paul-Michel Foucault, describes how certain ideas take on the power of a dominant discourse or "regime of truth"[102] that is hard to shake off because it has become a part of the self. Indeed, other scholars and observers have noticed how Singaporeans expect themselves to be highly competitive, economically independent, self-reliant, and active in the reproduction of their own well-being.[103] They self-regulate and upgrade themselves, learn new skills, and stay relevant to avoid unemployment.[104]

Indeed, none of the parents in my research ever mentioned the alternate, imagined reality of a more egalitarian society; or, God forbid, one in which the quest for economic rewards does not form the primary basis for life decisions. While the young people of Generation Z may change this worldview eventually, the overriding logic in Singapore still seems to revolve around being competitive and economically viable. Annexed to this is the belief that meritocratic principles of selection and incentivisation must be retained. There is no real alternative to meritocracy, claimed Lawrence Wong, then

Acting Minister for Culture, Community and Youth in 2013. Rather, "the challenge for us is to improve our system of meritocracy".[105]

> But what of you, my child?
> Daughter, future, hope.
>
> What of me, Mother?
> My path is paved with the lavender lullabies
> you sung in the bath at bedtime.

The persistent ironies were not lost on me. I was, on the one hand, a local Singaporean teacher who espoused a more open-ended and less rote-based methodology in the classroom. I was also a woman with multiple degrees and certifications and yet, one who agonised deeply over the educational rat race and its effects on children's hearts and minds. Last—and this is perhaps where life plays its most sardonic hand—I was not prepared to see my own children fail to secure educational and (some kind of) economic success of their own.

Perhaps this is a further testament to the influence of "governmentality" in the "conduct of (our) conduct".[106] In spite of my own passionate ideals, I was, in the end, nothing more than a pragmatic Singaporean whose own daughters had received their fair share of tuition classes and many, many more hours of enrichment activities over the course of their childhood and schooling.

Conflicted? Confused? Hypocritical?

Well, I firmly believed—and still do—in the power of creative play and tangible experiences to transform young lives. I still believe in the inherent value of that **one** individual child, and that good quality early education can have positive and beneficial effects on future outcomes. Press me further and I can (but may not) rattle off names of Wee Care students who went on to enter gifted and talented programmes around the world. Some have received scholarships, including those from the Public Service Commission (PSC), Singapore.

Indeed, the research evidence exists to support the importance of play for young children. In classrooms with developmentally appropriate practices (DAP), boys have been shown to suffer less stress while concomitantly demonstrating increased motivation and emotional development.[107] In one study in Northern Ireland, children who learnt within the framework of a developmentally appropriate curriculum—especially when there was a good balance between adult-initiated and child-initiated activities—were more motivated and attentive; plus, they displayed higher-order thinking and multiple skills acquisition.[108] In another study, children who had been taught according to the Tools of the Mind syllabus (a programme inspired by the ideas of the Russian psychologist, Lev Vygotsky) showed improvements in executive functioning such as working memory and cognitive flexibility.[109]

There are good, sound, and empirically valid reasons for pursuing progressive learning practices in early childhood. But in the first 10 years after Wee Care's founding, this was not always understood or recognised: that children do not necessarily lose out by playing. Indeed, children can (and should) play, grow, learn, be happy, and become successful in their own ways, in their chosen interests, in their respective spheres of influence.

Exacerbating the ideological mismatch I was confronted with was the mix of clients Wee Care had begun to serve too. The cultural differences led to interesting dynamics at times and I had to become a bit of a cultural chameleon while simultaneously striving to establish consistency and integrity across all of our practices. Not just how much to learn or play, but over everything from the kinds of snacks we offered to the unbiased stories we read, from the way consent forms for outings were drafted to the frequency and modalities of communication we had with parents. It was all quite nerve-wracking at times because the multicultural and multinational mix meant that misunderstandings were an ever-present possibility.

Slowly and painfully though, we started to beat the competition ourselves. Enrolment grew and the company managed to, somehow, shake off its birth pangs. By the time we moved to our new centre near the Botanic Gardens, Wee Care had to register for the Goods and Services Tax (GST) and all of our clients, regardless of ethnicity or nationality, were keen to have their children learn through play **and** achieve academic excellence, an ongoing phenomenon that I can only attribute to competition in the global economy. Where this struggle involves education especially, we can thank league tables and international achievement tests like the Programme for International Student Assessment (PISA) for contributing to the enduring anxieties.

92   Ludington-Hoe, S., & Golant, S. K. (1987). *How to have a smarter baby: The infant stimulation program for enhancing your baby's natural development.* New York, NY: Bantam Books.

93   This is an authoritarian form of parenting that is strict or demanding, where the children are pushed and pressured to achieve high levels of academic success and/or be proficient in extracurricular activities such as music or sports. For more on this, see Kim, S. Y. (2013, July). What is "tiger" parenting? How does it affect children? *Developmental Psychologist.* http://www.apadivisions.org/division-7/publications/newsletters/developmental/2013/07/tiger-parenting

94   Low, D. (2014). Good meritocracy, bad meritocracy. In D. Low & S. T. Vadaketh (Eds.), *Hard choices: Challenging the Singapore consensus* (pp. 48–58). Singapore: NUS Press.

95   Tan, K. P. (2008). Meritocracy and elitism in a global city: Ideological shifts in Singapore. *International Political Science Review, 29*(1), 7–27.

96   Ng, P. T. (2008). Thinking schools, learning nation. In J. Tan & P. T. Ng (Eds.), *Thinking schools, learning nation: Contemporary issues and challenges* (pp. 1–6). Singapore: Pearson Prentice Hall.

97   Tan, K. P. (2008). Meritocracy and elitism in a global city: Ideological shifts in Singapore. *International Political Science Review, 29*(1), 7–27.

98   Gestwicki, C. (2014). *Developmentally appropriate practice: Curriculum and development in early education* (5th ed.). Belmont, CA: Wadsworth Cengage Learning.

99   Gestwicki, C. (2014). *Developmentally appropriate practice: Curriculum and development in early education* (5th ed.). Belmont, CA: Wadsworth Cengage Learning.

100 Chua, M. L. D. (2016). *A critical study of academic acceleration in the early years in Singapore.* [Doctoral thesis, University College London]. UCL Discovery. https://discovery.ucl.ac.uk/id/eprint/1521017/

101 Foucault, M. (2003). Technologies of the self. In P. Rabinow & N. Rose (Eds.), *The essential Foucault: Selections from essential works of Foucault, 1954–1984* (pp. 145–169). New York: New Press.

102 Foucault, M. (1980). Truth and power. In C. Gordon (Ed.), *Power/Knowledge: Selected interviews and other writings, 1972–1977* (pp. 109–133). (C. Gordon, L. Marshall, J. Mepham, & K. Soper, Trans.). New York: Pantheon Books. Also, see Foucault, M. (1980). Two lectures. In C. Gordon (Ed.), Power / Knowledge: Selected interviews and other writings, 1972–1977 (pp. 78–108). (C. Gordon, L. Marshall, J. Mepham, & K. Soper, Trans.). New York: Pantheon Books.

103 Liow, E. D. (2009). *Reconstructing the working class: Neoliberalism and retail workers in Singapore.* [Master's thesis, National University of Singapore]. ScholarBank@NUS. https://scholarbank.nus.edu.sg/handle/10635/18201

104 Liow, E. D. (2012). The neoliberal-developmental state: Singapore as case study. *Critical Sociology, 38*(2), 241–264. Also see Yap, S. H. (2012). The "Government" in our lives: An exploratory study of ideology and the Singapore middle class [Unpublished final year project]. Nanyang Technological University, Singapore. https://hdl.handle.net/10356/87281

105 Toh, E. (2013, January 28). No alternative to meritocracy, says Lawrence Wong. *The Straits Times.* https://www.straitstimes.com/singapore/no-alternative-to-meritocracy-says-lawrence-wong

106 Foucault, M. (2003). Technologies of the self. In P. Rabinow & N. Rose (Eds.), *The essential Foucault: Selections from essential works of Foucault, 1954–1984* (pp. 145–169). New York: New Press.
107 Dunn, L. & Kontos, S. (1997). What have we learned about developmentally appropriate practice? Research in Review. *Young Children, 52*(5), 4–13. See also Van Horn, L. M., Karlin, E. O., Ramey, S. L., Aldridge, J., & Snyder, S. W. (2005). Effects of developmentally appropriate practices on children's development: A review of research and discussion of methodological and analytic issues. *The Elementary School Journal, 105*(4), 325–351.
108 McGuinness, C., Sproule, L., Trew, K., & Walsh, G. (2009). *The Early Years Enriched Curriculum Evaluation Project (EYECEP) End-of-Phase 2, Report 2 Inside EC classrooms and schools: Children, teachers and school principals.* Belfast, N. Ireland: Council for the Curriculum, Examinations & Assessment (CCEA). https://pdfs.semanticscholar.org/ac2d/c8af3d781a27ade76c9d9d009affed9636dd.pdf
109 Diamond, A., Barnett, W. S., Thomas, J., & Munro, S. (2007). Preschool program improves cognitive control. *Science, 318*(5855), 1387–1388.

8

NAVIGATING BLAME AND RESPONSIBILITY

WHY didn't you tell me? Why? WHY didn't you tell me that Noah caught the chickenpox? Don't you know that the year-end examinations are coming up soon? This will affect Jasmine's results. What am I going to do? What will happen if she gets chickenpox and can't sit for the exams? Don't you care? What's wrong with you?!

The accusations came fast and furious. As I read the email, I felt my heart drop and pound simultaneously. Waves of sadness—now a familiar but uninvited friend—swept over me like a heavy blanket and then, without warning, a burst of other emotions gushed in; opposing feelings of anger and indignation that threatened to destroy the walls of my inner self, that prideful sanctum, that hidden space where the human soul seeks to find its balance and joy, and yet, the very place where often it sheds its secret tears, only to build new and fortified walls to keep the enemies of destruction in ... and out.

What am I do to with all of this anger, Lord? Where can I dump it? I do not want it. I do not want any more of this.

But there was more, much more. She refused to hear out my explanations, or maybe she did hear them but would not accept the genuine innocence of the reasoning. "Most children now are vaccinated against chickenpox. It never once crossed my mind that Jasmine and Julianna have not been vaccinated, plus I had no idea Noah sits next to Julianna on the school bus."

"Those reasons are just not good enough," she spat back vehemently. "You've now cost my child her exam results. If it were not for the fact that Julianna is about to graduate from your preschool, you can be sure I will have her withdrawn. All parents should hear of this."

She did precisely that. I was mortified to learn within the week that, in spite of my attempts to explain things, she contacted an evening tabloid about the supposed "outbreak" of chickenpox in the school. Without checking the facts or interviewing me, the newspaper subsequently ran a feature of the incident. It suggested that the principal had been negligent.

Could there have been a more destructive indictment? What negligence? When all day, every day, we hold and hug, cajole and persuade, remind and nag, nag, nag ourselves, each other, the children: be careful, careful, careful ... don't run, don't push, don't fall .... Don't— because we love you. We really do ... you are, almost as much as your mother's, our child too.

I had somehow considered her an ally in earlier times. She had been so kind to us, so supportive of our programmes and events that her outburst was nothing but uncharacteristic, shocking, and thoroughly unexpected. I had been on her mailing list of "friends", in fact. Her small business had failed a year or so prior and I had been amongst the circle of recipients sharing in her stress and sorrows. What had changed? Had the teachers and I been careless in other ways that she had immediately assumed ill will on my part in not informing her quickly about the chickenpox case? I wanted to tell her—so much—that I had, in fact, been keeping watch on the matter, that I was waiting to see if there was just cause for raising an alarm; that we had had sporadic cases of chickenpox in the past with no spread to other students. But I was given very little chance to speak and after a while, something in me just collapsed.

I have thought of you many times over the years, often with pain. How are you? Julianna and Jasmine must be young ladies now. Are you well? Are they well?

She was, unfortunately, not the last. A few years after, the school administrator came to my office early one morning to inform me that one of the little girls in the pre-nursery class had been stopped in the reception lobby for having two little red dots on one of her feet. We could not be sure, at the time, if it was Hand-Foot-Mouth Disease (HFMD) as spots can mean anything, or nothing. Moreover, the infection is almost imperceptible in the early stages. From experience, however, I knew that a child who begins to show HFMD symptoms in, say, the afternoon, would most certainly have been contagious in the morning (and often, with no obvious symptoms). Feeling that I had little choice in the matter, I called the girl's mother to ask if she would please come to take her daughter to the doctor for a more informed diagnosis. The mother seemed stressed and upset over the phone, but this was understandable. No parent ever wants their child to be sick.

She marched in, angry, like she had been thinking about the disease in all of the fifteen minutes it had taken her to arrive at Wee Care. "This is all your fault," she began. "Are you sure it is HFMD? How can you be sure? It's a very serious illness. I have heard that other children have died from this disease before."

I willed myself to stay calm. "I cannot be sure," I explained, "but it would be best for you to have your daughter checked by a doctor. It can be very mild in some children."

"No, no, no," she responded. "How can you say that?"

And then the dam burst. She began screaming, hysterically, at me, for causing the HFMD, for being mean, for not caring, for everything. She screamed and screamed and screamed. Her husband came, angry with me too, but understood and tried to get her to leave with him so that their little girl could be taken to the doctor. But she would not budge. The screams penetrated my mind, my soul, until all I could do was to breathe and wait, wait and breathe.

Breathe ... breathe ... breathe .... It will end ... maybe ... no ....

She screamed for more than an hour, non-stop. Outside my office, my staff were beginning to worry. They were looking at me, waiting for a signal to act, but how? One of them tried to intervene but I stopped her with a firm look.

If anyone is going to get hurt, it will be me, not you.

I wondered if any of the parents arriving to pick their children up at morning dismissal could hear her. It did not seem that she would be able to stop screaming on her own. Finally, I found the physical strength to get up from my desk and open the door. "Call the police," I said. They did not have to come. She stopped and left within five minutes of this instruction.

In the afternoon, I received a sweet and calm email from her, saying that the doctor had indeed confirmed it was HFMD and that I should inform the rest of the preschool parents. I chose not to respond, probably because I was still nursing a sore chest from her verbal tirade in the morning. The next day, I received a call from the Ministry of Education.

"You probably know why I am calling," the inspector began.
"Yes, of course."
"So, what happened?"
I explained.
"Why did she say you showed her the door?"
"I didn't show her the door. I got up to open my office door because she said her husband was coming."
Silence, and then laughter from the inspector.
"Well, all right then. I will let her know."

I have blocked her out of my mind since. But once in a while, the memory returns and I wonder. How is your little girl? She must be a young lady now.

In workplace settings that receive a high volume of customer traffic, there is sometimes a notice placed in prominent view. The notice states that aggressive or abusive forms of behaviour by anyone towards service staff will not be tolerated under any circumstance; that the company values its staff and requires that they be respected. It is a reasonable request. Service staff are correspondingly expected to be helpful, polite, kind, and empathic towards their clients.

But I never wanted a sign like that at Wee Care and for many reasons; primarily because I think it is wrong to be defensive and warn someone off without first understanding the reasons for the person's stressed behaviour. Secondly, because most of the time, parents are supportive and appreciative of the love and care we extend to their children. It was also my personal conviction and pedagogical aim that teachers and parents should regard themselves as co-labourers, partners in the important work to raise healthy, happy, and well-adjusted children. To me, then and now, teaching is enacted through and in relationship. You cannot teach a child outside of the relationship you have with him/her. The same applies within the iterative relationships that you have with the child's parents, and the parents with the child.

The research literature tells us that the ideal family-school relationship is one with a child-centred connection where the adults in the home and school both share responsibility for supporting the child's growth and development. In addition, a healthy parent-teacher relationship is often distinguished by shared beliefs and mutual efforts to sustain the relationship as well as establish consistency and continuity in practices across both the home and school settings. Only these will promote the child's adjustment.[110]

Researchers have also found that a number of factors contribute to the success of family-school relationships. These include relational trust between the families and schools, respect and personal regard for the other, accountability, consideration, sensitivity, and understanding, plus equality and reciprocity.[111] When these relationships are characterised by mutuality, connectedness, and congruence, they serve to build intentional and collaborative partnerships.[112]

Importantly, good parent-teacher relationships do not develop automatically. They evolve over time and form stable patterns, expectations, and a quality that is quite distinct from the interactions themselves.[113] Indeed, I can recall conversations where a parent and I may not have completely agreed on a matter. Yet, the relationship was able to develop in spite of the divergence and later, realign once more on other topics. In a way, most healthy relationships are like this.

Significantly, the **quality** of the parent-teacher relationship is more predictive of child outcomes than the amount of contact between parents and teachers.[114] Subtle variables between the parent and the child, as well as between the parent and the teacher, can strongly influence the parent's decision to become involved in school along with the exact outcomes achieved through the engagement.[115] At Wee Care, the little things did matter a lot. Parents appreciated welcoming smiles from me and the teachers; others needed more frequent email updates ... and yet others told me to stop bothering them with unnecessary emails!

Indeed, because positive family-school relationships are valuable and beneficial, we spent a great deal of time at Wee Care building (what we believed to be) trust and communication with all of our parents. We welcomed them, for example, to attend the Saturday playgroup sessions with their toddlers. In these sessions, there would be circle time, imaginative and sensory forms of play, group games as well as mutual discussions around the snack table. It was an incredibly effective way to get to know the children as individuals, and their parents for their worldviews, opinions, attitudes, and concerns. Inversely, the families were equally able to "see" into our hearts, week after week, through our actions and words; to get to know us, so to speak, including our personalities, values, and approaches to teaching.

After the child's entry to school, our teachers were expected to keep in close contact with parents through telephone or email updates. I also crafted termly newsletters and (where time permitted) weekly or monthly "Highlights" about the various lessons, activities, and experiences we had enjoyed in the different age groups, subject areas, or classrooms. Without a doubt, there were many opportunities for parents to get involved at Wee Care—from participating in field trips and attending special events to Project Days, as well as our annual Cultural Day when we would turn the tables and ask parents to come and tell us about their own culture or heritage instead. We amassed a broad perspective just looking and listening to these presentations. The cultural practices featured came from as far afield as Scandinavia to our very own Peranakan customs. They ranged from sampling Korean rice cakes and Russian blinis to competing—hands behind back—for Indonesian *kerupuk*˙.

But these efforts were not always enough.

I could hear the happy hum of activities emanating down the corridor to my office, telling me that school was in full swing. And then the shriek ... and then another. Through the clear glass panel on my door, I saw a mother bolt down the corridor. She was shrieking something but I could not hear the words. I rushed out, thinking that something terrible must have happened.

She was screaming now, screaming into the face of one of our supporting staff members, an elderly aide in the pre-nursery classroom. I intervened to ask what was wrong and the mother turned and vented her rage on me.

"She didn't let him go! She didn't let him go!"

I was puzzled but tried to piece the story together as quickly as I could. The mother—a new parent whose child had just started school for the first time that week—had crept into the school corridor from the main lobby before classes were dismissed. She had managed to do this because the school manager had stepped away from the front desk for a few minutes, probably to use the bathroom. Upon seeing

---

˙ This is a starch-based deep-fried cracker that is flavoured by other ingredients such as fish, prawns, or garlic. It originates from Indonesia (particularly from Javanese cuisine) but has become popular in South East Asian countries.

her son lining up with the rest of his class, she had shouted out to him cheerfully that she had arrived to pick him up. The boy, who was still in the throes of separation anxiety, burst into tears upon seeing her and then attempted to dash towards her along the corridor. The aide, worried that he might slip and fall, held on to one of his hands. This led to a short struggle, a struggle that the mother interpreted as evil, controlling, and painful.

Later, I was to comfort and counsel the aide who wept in my office wondering what she had done wrong. I was also to chide the father who called a while later and threatened that if Wee Care could not go along with what he and his wife wanted, they would pull their son out of the programme. I politely agreed that that would probably be the best for all concerned, a response that he probably did not expect as he remained silent thereafter.

A few hours later, the mother returned, calmer and apologetic, to pick up her son's belongings. She asked the manager on duty why the aide had not let her son go. The manager replied to say that the class had been baking that morning and the laminate floor was somewhat greasy from the butter that had been used.

The aide was just worried your son might slip and fall.

I used to wonder why interpersonal incidents like these occurred at school. I used to think the teachers or I had done something wrong, or that we had not done enough, or that we had not communicated sufficiently. Conflicts were especially maddening when a teacher's act of responsibility was misconstrued as being uncaring or unkind. Once, a mother complained that I had not compelled her child to sit down on the floor with the rest of the class. The little boy had chosen to sit on a chair at the table just next to the group. He had seemed very happy and was still listening to the story, so I had decided to leave him there. To me, it mattered more that he was happy and learning, than how his body reclined in space.

Invariably though, differences such as these, especially when accompanied by anger or the child's withdrawal from the school, start to take a toll. The feeling of being unappreciated and misunderstood is a very real threat to the teacher's sense of security and well-being at work. But more damaging than this—even when I tried to brush things off and/or reduce disagreements down to a mere "cultural difference"—the awful realisation was that, in the eyes of some families, Wee Care teachers and I would **always and never** be more than paid service staff. According to this worldview, relationships are consumerist and transactional; "the customer is always right" and we do what the customer wants. In turn, our effort or "the service" is judged for its economic utility, whether it meets and satisfies the customer's needs and expectations or not.

This supposition was not mere conjecture. I found confirming evidence, many years later in my doctoral research, that parents use a cost-benefit analysis when evaluating the worth of a preschool programme, even when the lessons are free! One mother, for instance, revealed that she had evaluated her child's learning centre along numerous criteria, including its physical space and the quality of lighting in the classrooms, the teacher-student ratio, the ways in which lessons were conducted, what sorts of skills would be learnt, ease of access (including parking and traffic), and whether the staff in the centre were friendly. Another mother said that she had withdrawn her daughter from programmes where she had felt "frustrated", where she had not been sure the lessons were achieving anything. Other parents listed teacher characteristics—including accountability, flexibility, and feedback—as crucial factors in their evaluation of economic utility, down to the very accents the teachers had. On the flip side, when lessons were provided by a charity or not-for-profit organisation, the parents made less demands; but only because they knew—and said—that they should not expect too much. In a paradoxical way, they drew their interpretations of quality and service from a consumerist framework still. They were "not customers" but recipients of goodwill.

But eh, do not be a hypocrite. You are a parent too. You have done the same, assessed teachers and programmes as good or bad depending on how much money you had to pay for them.

Neoliberalism changes the philosophical foundation and sociocultural practices of education because schooling becomes a "quasi-market" or "free market" where parents and children are recreated as consumers and educational programmes, commodities.[116] The psychological impact of this on teachers is real and significant. In my research, kindergarten teachers indicated that they often felt constrained and voiceless; they could not act as they thought best for the child because they were private employees only, service providers in this busy "marketplace".

In the same vein, kindergartens begin to regulate themselves too. A culture of self-interest can develop where there is a move away from social or educational concerns, including a resistance to having inclusive classrooms where children with different needs may be viewed as lowering standards for the entire class or school.[117] For myself, personally, I know that I have capitulated to providing more second language lessons, organic food, room thermometers (to keep classroom temperatures just right), personalised emails ... the list goes on, all to please one parent or another.

But please do not get me wrong. Many early childhood educators have a heart to serve and support their families and students.

However, the freedom of choice that is a much-lauded feature of a free market, the freedom that allows a parent to complain and/or withdraw his/her child at the smallest of slights, can effectively destroy the teacher's soul.[118] I know I am not alone in feeling this.[119]

Furthermore, at the macro level, there are real reasons to fear when a country's education policies allow "profits to be made from the privatisation of education".[120] An "entrepreneurial government"[121] may really be benefitting from not investing much needed public funds to improve the quality of education for all children and, I would emphasise here, their teachers. To date, with the exception of 28 MOE Kindergartens as well as partial schemes to subsidise the operational costs of a few "preferred operators", early childhood education in Singapore is still largely unfunded by the state.[122] In contrast, publicly funded and free preschool is available in many European countries such as Denmark, Germany, Belgium, Norway, Sweden, and the United Kingdom. In Finland, not only is preschool education completely free-of-charge, the children also receive a free meal during the school day plus free transport if he/she lives far away or in a more inaccessible area.[123]

Indeed, many international advocates for early childhood education unanimously agree that quality preschool education is invariably publicly or government-funded rather than left to the private sector.[124] In 2012, the Organisation for Economic Cooperation and Development (OECD) reported that school choice and the mechanisms of an educational marketplace tend to increase segregation and inequities in and across schools.[125] Why? Simply because wealthy families are able to give their children access to higher-quality schools which, by circumstance (i.e. higher rents, higher salaries, better-quality school materials, and learning experiences), are also more expensive settings to operate. It grieved me considerably that in order to sustain the quality of education and care we were providing at Wee Care, school fees had to be raised (from 2004 annually) until—compared at the per-hourly rate—we were one of the most expensive preschools in Singapore to attend.

---

110 Clarke, B. L., Sheridan, S. M., & Woods, K. E. (2010). Elements of healthy family-school relationships. In S. L. Christenson & A. L. Reschly (Eds.), *Handbook of school-family partnerships* (pp. 61–79). New York: Routledge.
111 Bryk, A. S., & Schneider, B. L. (2002). *Trust in schools: A core resource for improvement.* New York: Russell Sage Foundation. See also Minke, K. M. (2006). Parent-teacher relationships. In G. G. Bear & K. M. Minke (Eds.), *Children's needs III: Development, prevention, and intervention* (pp. 73–85). Washington, D.C.: National Association of School Psychologists.
112 Christenson, S. L. & Sheridan, S. M. (2001). *Schools and families: Creating essential connections for learning.* New York: The Guildford Press. See also Dinnebeil, L. A., Hale, L. M., & Rule, S. (1996). A qualitative analysis of parents' and service coordinators' descriptors of variables that influence collaborative relationships. *Topics in Early Childhood Special Education, 16*(3), 322–347; and Dinnebeil, L. A., Hale, L. M., & Rule, S. (1999). Early intervention program practices that support collaboration. *Topics in Early Childhood Special Education, 19*(4), 225–235.
113 Pianta, R. C., & Walsh, D. J. (1996). *High-risk children in schools: Constructing sustaining relationships.* New York: Routledge.
114 Kohl, G. O., Lengua, L. J., & McMahon, R. J. (2000). Parent involvement in school: Conceptualising multiple dimensions and their relations with family and demographic risk factors. *Journal of School Psychology, 38*(6), 501–523.
115 Jeynes, W. H. (2011). *Parental involvement and academic success.* New York: Routledge.
116 Lee, I-F. (2012). Unpacking neoliberal policies: Interrupting the global and local production of the norms. *Journal of Pedagogy, 3*(1), 30–42.
117 Ball, S. J. (2008). *The education debate* (2nd ed.). Bristol, UK: The Policy Press.
118 Walker, A. (2003). *In search of our mothers' gardens: Womanist prose.* Orlando, FL: Harcourt Brace. See also Palmer, P. J. (2017). *The courage to teach: Exploring the inner landscape of a teacher's life (20th anniversary ed.).* San Francisco, CA: Jossey Bass.
119 Ong, T. (2019, March 5). Husband of early childhood teacher in Singapore reveals wife's 6 years of unseen teaching sacrifices. *Mothership.* https://mothership.sg/2019/03/husband-early-childhood-teacher-sacrifices-teaching/
120 Ball, S. J. (2008). *The education debate* (2nd ed.). Bristol, UK: The Policy Press.
121 Osborne, D., & Gaebler, T. (1993). *Reinventing government: How the entrepreneurial spirit is transforming the public sector.* New York, NY: Plume.

122 For more information on MOE Kindergartens, see Ministry of Education, Singapore. (n.d.). *Overview of MOE Kindergarten.* https://moe.gov.sg/preschool/moe-kindergarten/overview/
For information about Anchor Operators, see Early Childhood Development Agency. (n.d.). *ECDA Anchor Operator Scheme (AOP).* https://www.ecda.gov.sg/Parents/Pages/AOP.aspx
For information about Partner Operators, see Early Childhood Development Agency. (n.d.). *ECDA Partner Operator Scheme (POP).* https://www.ecda.gov.sg/Parents/Pages/POP.aspx
123 For more information about Finland, see Kumpulainen, T. (Ed.) (2018). *Key figures on early childhood and basic education in Finland 2018.* Helsinki, Finland: Finnish National Agency for Education. https://www.oph.fi/en/statistics-and-publications/publications/key-figures-early-childhood-and-basic-education-finland
Another quick resource may be found at InfoFinland. (n.d.). *Preschool education.* https://www.infofinland.fi/en/living-in-finland/education/child-education/preschool-education
124 Ang, L. (2012). *Vital voices for vital years: A study of leaders' perspectives on improving the early childhood sector in Singapore.* Singapore: Lien Foundation.
125 OECD (2012). *Equity and quality in education: Supporting disadvantaged students and schools.* Paris: OECD Publishing. https://www.oecd.org/education/school/50293148.pdf

9

BRAVING DROUGHT AND FAMINE

> "I want to learn how to hold the paradoxical poles of my identity together, to embrace the profoundly opposite truths that my sense of self is deeply dependent on others dancing with me and that I still have a sense of self when no one wants to dance."[126]

In the early days at Wee Care, I had to do just about anything and everything for the company. The business was not productive enough to afford cleaners and other "nice-to-have" staff like receptionists or assistant teachers. Hence, I swept when the floor needed to be swept, and answered the phone when it rang. At different times, I served as a Baby Buddy or a therapist, a playgroup leader or a preschool teacher (especially when teachers called in sick or worse, quit without notice), and often in addition to my other roles managing the company, which became more and more differentiated and demanding as the years wore on and the company grew.

If my memory serves me right, I taught Saturday playgroup sessions (including infant playgroups and the afternoon social skills playgroup for children with special needs) to 2015, some 15 or 16 years after Wee Care ran its first toddler playgroup sessions at its fledgling Thomson Road site. Moreover, save for a few years when we had a dedicated Clinical Supervisor heading up our programmes in early intervention, I supported our team of behavioural and educational therapists too, vetting Individual Educational Plans (IEPs) and video footage frequently, in addition to meeting up with the children's parents to review progress.

Indeed, before specific tasks could be handed over to actual employees (and sometimes even after!), I was the go-to Girl Friday who stepped up and filled in for someone or something, sometimes at very short notice. This is not to discount the reality that there were other trusted souls within my teaching team who would, and did in fact, do the same. But I think I remember this aspect of my working life at Wee Care like a PTSD* flashback. It was not easy.

I often comforted myself with a joke in my head that I was gaining worthwhile experiences as a tour guide (which I became very good at in the course of handling field trips), emergency nurse (when children fell ill or sustained injuries), mediator (defusing squabbles between children and sometimes between staff), actress, singer and emcee (during school performances), interior designer and gardener (for our indoor and outdoor spaces), along with the more conventional responsibilities in curriculum development, human resource management, accounts and finance (which I was miserable at), and marketing (which I never mastered either, particularly when

---

*   An acronym for Post-Traumatic Stress Disorder.

social media became the mainstay)! The intense busy-ness of those days kept me very humble **and** very tired.

But understandably and as a direct result, I was always very grateful and excited whenever a new employee came on board who could potentially be able to take some of the load off me. Looking back, Wee Care and I were incredibly blessed to have a team of able, dedicated, and faithful men and women join our ranks to serve as teachers, therapists, and managers. They sang and danced, read and painted, wiped and mopped, ran and squatted, scolded and encouraged, lifted and sorted—continuously, without complaining (okay, maybe some), and for less pay than they should have received, and considerably less recognition and status than they deserved.

You know who you are but for what it is worth,

Eileen, Jeannie, Ratna, Jayne, Luci, and Faith,
Zahrin, Rose, Mel, Tara, and Nellyn,
Susan, Cherie,
Ritu, Renee, Richel, and Sheren,
Nicole, Jon, James, Yan Jie, and Siti—

thank you so much, from the very bottom of my heart.

These and other Wee Care Warriors were the exception rather than the rule though. We did not have **a** problem with human resources. We had many.

For one, it was incredibly difficult to find teachers with the qualifications, experience, and willingness to serve in our programmes. If you recall, Wee Care at the outset was neither a childcare centre or a kindergarten strictly. So a kindergarten teacher might apply for a position and then discover at the interview that she would be needed to teach in playgroup classes on Saturday mornings. Or she might be told she would not be accorded the same holidays or term breaks as the children but have a pre-determined quota of annual leave instead.

When we did manage to secure staff, they were usually fresh university graduates who were willing to learn but who needed to be trained from scratch. As one would expect, being young and inexperienced had its benefits but also, distinct disadvantages. Open-minded and energetic, our new teachers made their fair (large) share of mistakes which parents sometimes misread as signs of laziness, a lack of care or competence, or outright negligence.

Look at her email! It's ridiculously long and vacuous! How can she expect us to read updates like this?

Can you please tell Teacher Hope to make sure Lucas finishes up everything in his thermos flask? Yes, he has to eat all of the rice and soup, plus the fruit. It's not too much.

For a while, the only way Wee Care managed to find enough teachers was to employ teachers from overseas. Given the employment laws in place at that time, we were able to secure teachers from Indonesia, China, and the Philippines, even Myanmar and India; and frankly, I really enjoyed collaborating with these teachers. They were earnest and hard-working, and I respected them for their courage and willingness to learn.

These hires, however, tended to generate problems of a different kind. Even though many of these individuals were university graduates, differences in accent, culture, and/or working style sometimes led to tensions and/or misunderstandings. There was also the problem of homesickness or the ever-present possibility that health problems or family issues might cause the teacher to suddenly turn tail and leave. There was one teacher, for example, who claimed that she was stopping work to look after her family. A year later, we discovered that she had left Singapore without paying her income tax. The school had no choice but to settle the liability. Then there was the case of a teacher from one part of Asia who detested a teacher from another part of Asia because the latter was "too demanding, not nice, so rude". I found this description quite hard to believe, to be honest, and did not insist on the first teacher staying when she resigned.

Whatever the potential gambles and failings in making the right call, the bottom line for me was hiring staff with the right hearts rather than the right credentials per se. In this, I reasoned that qualifications and skills could always be taught; integrity, commitment, and love, however, could not be bought.

This is not to say that training is not important. Rather, there must be a good fit—at the very "minimum"—between the individual's character, temperament, and interests with the role and responsibilities of being an early childhood educator. Unfortunately, in Singapore, the dominant approach by the government has always been about raising the "minimum academic qualifications of preschool teachers"[127] than cultivating the teacher's heart and soul, and addressing structural inequities in salaries and professional status.

Denise, Teacher Vicky has barricaded herself in the classroom.

Huh? Why?

Well, Principal Sarah has been trying to get her to finish writing up her lesson plans. She seems to have taken a personal offence to this.

Oh, for goodness sake.

Denise, can you hear me?

Yes, what's wrong? Why aren't you on leave? It's Christmas and I am in Taiwan.

Denise, Teacher Vicky came to return her uniforms yesterday.

Okay...?

She punched Assistant Teacher Lily on the arm.

What? Why?

She's angry about everything; she says that we have not shown her respect, that we have been unfair to her.

In what way have we been unfair to her? That's unreasonable.

She's gone off to make a police report that we started the altercation.

That's ridiculous. Assistant Teacher Lily is 60 years old! Check the CCTV cameras to see if we have the incident on tape.

Okay, Denise, don't worry. We are trying our best here. Lily is shaken with some bruises but she is generally all right.

I learnt later that the most productive and least stressed preschool teachers incorporate personality traits such as sociability and physical energy, empathy and an orientation towards structure and details, high expectations of self and others, as well as a preference for reflection and direct communication.[128] In this, our use of the Birkman Method,[129] which we introduced at Wee Care around 2011, did much to explicate the nuances of teacher dispositions in hiring and cultivating strong and happy educators, and competent and effective teams.

Indeed, before Birkman, managing preschool staff sometimes felt like walking on eggshells. While bad eggs were rare, this did not provide me with much solace as there were many more (sometimes vulnerable) individuals to care for. There were teachers, for instance, who had thought that teaching would be right for them but who ended up discovering—sometimes too late—that their personalities and occupational profiles suited them doing something else completely different.

Denise, Teacher Pat has not shown up for work.
Did she call in?
No.
Have you tried calling her?
Yes. The phone line is dead.

Denise, Teacher Pat has not come to work again.
Have you tried calling her?
Yes, the phone line is still dead.

Denise, what should we do with Teacher Pat's things? It does not look like she will be coming back.
Who's handling the class?
We're all taking turns till a new teacher can be hired.

There were (and still are) systemic causes to such mismatches. Entry into tertiary courses in Singapore is highly competitive and greatly dependent on meeting cut-off scores in large-scale national assessments such as the "O" or "A" level examinations. If a student fails to gain entry into, say, a preferred course such as psychology, the next best step would be to consider other—hopefully related—courses with lower prerequisites. As the thinking goes, gaining admission into a less favoured course would be a better option than not getting any tertiary qualification at all, a logic that begets the possibility of "poor fits" when these students finally graduate and begin working.

This situation is further compounded by the fact that the "minimum academic qualifications" to becoming a government-registered early childhood educator in Singapore has always been set relatively low.[130] Even today, one need only obtain five "O" level passes to qualify, with a B4 grade in English and a C6 in Mathematics, and where the main medium of instruction for all of these subjects, except for a language subject, must be English. In contrast, to qualify as an early childhood educator in Finland, an individual must complete a Bachelor's degree in Education and have at least 60 credits of studies towards professional competencies in early childhood education and care.[131]

Please do not think I am elitist. Wee Care welcomed teachers with lower credentials who eventually studied and worked their way to the relevant certificate, diploma, and even, degree. But the process started with their interest and a passion to serve. The opportunity to serve confirmed their interests and passion so that getting properly trained was the next best step, and a very natural one to take for that matter. Unfortunately, when the bar is set too low, it becomes too easy for an individual to launch him/herself down a completely unsuitable career path. When the bar is set higher (and when entry is competitive), one is forced to consider how interested one really is in the subject matter before investing the time, effort, and energy to secure the coveted qualification.

And again, please do not get me wrong. It is important that teachers in the classroom are trained and competent before being given the immense responsibility of caring for and educating young children. If we really and truly believed this though, then the bar for entry into the profession must be set higher—much, much higher—or we focus from the time our students are teenagers to helping them understand themselves and their passions better. I think we do our young people a great disservice when we, as a government, family, or school do not talk about intrinsic worth based on **who we are** but concentrate instead on what must be achieved. To this end and under close supervision, Wee Care welcomed older students as volunteers in our classrooms on a regular basis. In the early days, these students—some of them from international schools and volunteering in the afternoons or at the weekends—were instrumental and indispensable as our extra pairs of hands and legs, particularly for routine tasks such as washing hands, taking the children to and from the toilet, and/or moving the children up and down the stairs. I met many wonderful young people this way and still have fond memories of them.

People who discover that they are in the wrong jobs suffer the consequences, obviously, of their decisions. There may be significant regret and disappointment, and also a sense of failure or of having wasted valuable time. But the consequences do not end there. There are repercussions felt by the preschool and the children/families too. A new teacher will need time to get to know the children and their needs, preferences, and personal idiosyncrasies. Knowledge that the former teacher had about a child or the class may not automatically transfer to the new teacher. The entire learning curve on both sides (teacher about family, and family about teacher) must begin all over again.

At the same time, the new teacher has to grapple with understanding the ethos, values, and practices in the new workplace.

The school will have to train (or rather, retrain) the fresh recruit in the organisation's unique processes and protocols; this teacher will need time to become familiar with them. Overall, every departure and every new hire in the early childhood field is a tough transition. Replacement costs are high and there may be staffing gaps before the new member of staff can come on board.[132]

Personally, it used to drive me crazy.

Denise, I am leaving because I am pregnant.
Denise, I am leaving because there is no one to look after my son.
Denise, I am leaving because you have not promoted me.
Denise, I am leaving because I want to try something new.
Denise, I am leaving because I don't want to work on Saturdays.
Denise, I am leaving ...

Turnover in the preschool sector in Singapore is very high.[133] One study has identified employee remuneration (i.e. low pay), employee benefits (i.e. few benefits), the work environment (i.e. stressful and tiring), and professional development opportunities (i.e. limited prospects for promotion) as factors affecting teacher retention in the early childhood context in Singapore.[134]

At the same time, recruitment is hampered by the perception that preschool work is a low-status occupation, or women's work, or low-skilled caring work that can be done without remuneration.[135] There were seasons, in fact, when I would receive only one or two résumés in response to a job advertisement; you can imagine the direct end result. Like any drought that leads to a famine, a shortage of teachers usually meant that we would not be able to open new classes, or worse, be forced to turn children away from an existing programme.

But from the teacher's perspective, I understood. The challenges of being a preschool teacher can add up to a very depressing state of affairs, both for someone considering it as a long-term career, or having been an early childhood teacher for a few years, suddenly finding herself "stuck" without much in terms of career progression to look forward to. Indeed, when you are surrounded by children all day, every day, with little recognition for all of your hard work and efforts, you begin to feel less confident and appealing, even to yourself!

But I could not and would not let high turnover undermine the school and affect the sense of stability that I knew our families and children needed. Around the time we introduced the Birkman Method, we overhauled our entire Human Resource system with the help of an external consultant, including the way we structured our wages and benefits. We introduced a slew of monetary and non-monetary benefits such as extra incentives for working on Saturdays and getting time-off in the afternoons. We linked Wee Care's vision, mission, and values to performance appraisals. We spent more time as a group, both in formal and informal settings, to nurture relationships, increase interpersonal understanding, and generally, build up our capabilities in working as a team. We surveyed staff satisfaction and addressed areas of concern as quickly as possible.

Did we succeed in solving the turnover problem at Wee Care? Yes and no.

Over the next few years, turnover at Wee Care did drop significantly. However, we still lost teachers to common problems such as a lack of "prospects", or the simple but troublesome fact that being largely female, many of the teachers faced life circumstances (involving elderly parents or children, or their physical health) that were just insurmountable.

And with regard to the former point, it was not that I was not willing to give my staff more opportunities for career growth. Rather, to achieve this objective, Wee Care would have had to engage in concerted and considerable business growth, year on year, to make meaningful job progression possible. We would have had to establish more schools so that more experienced staff could be placed in senior, supervisory positions; or we would have had to create more programmes, to increase the range of content areas the teachers could take on to learn new skills. Alternatively, we would have had to increase school fees or increase the student-to-teacher ratio in our classrooms to fund better remuneration and compensation packages.

It was such a horrible muddle most of the time. In my mind, more growth ran the risk of undermining the quality of care and education that I always wanted Wee Care to provide. Paradoxically too, it would have affected the quality of working life of my teachers. I wanted them to have time to smell the roses and smile at the children, not rush about their day teaching more and more classes; and I certainly did not want children herded about like cattle at school! I was also very reluctant to increase school fees. They were already very high; increasing them further would have alienated even more families from attending our programmes.

In the end, I came to the conclusion that the overall "business" environment for early childhood care and education in Singapore was a highly tenuous one. Any small shift in conditions could, and would, precipitate a dearth in enrolment or a storm of resignations. It felt like a constant battle against the elements, with the elements winning ever so often.

126 Palmer, P.J. (2017). *The courage to teach: Exploring the inner landscape of a teacher's life (20th anniversary ed.)*. San Francisco, CA: Jossey Bass.
127 Ministry of Education (2010). *Parliamentary reply: Motion on preschool education by the Minister of State, Ministry of Education, Mr. Masagos Zulkifli BMM*.
128 Wadlington, E., & Wadlington, P. (2011). Teacher dispositions: Implications for teacher education. *Childhood Education, 87*(5), 323–326.
129 For more information about the Birkman Method, please see Birkman International. (n.d.). https://birkman.com/
130 For more information, please see NIEC. (n.d.) *Diploma in Early Childhood Development & Education (N96 & T68)*. NIEC National Institute of Early Childhood Development. https://www.niec.edu.sg/courses/diplomas/early-childhood-development-education/
131 More information about this may be found at this site: Finnish National Agency for Education. (n.d.) *Qualification of teacher (early childhood education and care)*. https://www.suomi.fi/services/qualification-of-teacher-early-childhood-education-and-care-finnish-national-agency-for-education/45d6c503-95f5-41d7-8cdc-ba37fc73a240
132 Hausknecht, J. P., Rodda, J. M., & Howard, M. J. (2009). Targeted employee retention: Performance-based and job-related differences in reported reasons for staying. *Human Resource Management, 48*(2), 269–288.
133 Ang, L. (2012). *Vital voices for vital years: A study of leaders' perspectives on improving the early childhood sector in Singapore*. Singapore: Lien Foundation.
134 Pek-Greer, P., & Wallace, M. (2017). A study of childcare teacher retention in the childcare service industry. *Global Business Review, 18*(1), 71–86.
135 Folbre, N. (2003). Holding hands at midnight: The paradox of caring labor. In D. K. Barker & E. Kuiper (Eds.), *Toward a feminist philosophy of economics* (pp. 213–230). London: Routledge.

10

PLANTING MORE

> Numbers have a way of looking back at you
> with impunity
> saying nothing but
> piling mockery on your sweaty head
> saying nothing but
> indulging in the sweet pleasure of your discomforts
> while anguish weeps
> and pockets bleed,
> and quietly, the disaster of your downfall
> keeps getting closer.

I always dreaded looking at the company's balance sheets and profit-and-loss statements. As the year 2001 entered 2002 and then 2003 and 2004, the company's accumulated losses (or retained earnings) seemed to balloon bigger and bigger until it reached a staggering quarter of a million dollars. This was a figure so large and inconceivable to me that my heart would freeze whenever I thought of it.

Ironically, the school was growing. We were welcoming a steady stream of students into all of our programmes. Parents seemed to like what we were doing and we were getting new sign-ups on the basis of their regular and favourable word-of-mouth recommendations.

What many did not seem to realise, however, was that the costs of running the school were exorbitantly high. Every little bit seemed to add up, especially since we wanted to keep the student-to-teacher ratio low and especially because we were spending money on real and tangible learning materials instead of paper-and-pencil worksheets. The materials varied weekly and ranged from fruit and vegetables to ice and foam, and lots and lots of cardboard, poster board, paint, and fabric to recreate imaginary but lifelike play scenes each week.

Once, we made our playroom look like Japan. The children made maki, onigiri, and ramen. They smelt green tea and sampled Japanese crackers, scooped and poured uncooked rice, and observed goldfish swimming about in a small tank. In pretend play, they acted as Japanese rice farmers, "harvesting" imaginary stalks of rice from "fields" before loading and unloading "sacks" using toy wheelbarrows. They even "shopped" in a Japanese departmental store, trying on classic yukata and posing with paper umbrellas in hand.

As you can imagine, every ingredient, prop, or material in that week of lessons had to be made or purchased or both. It was hard work planning, organising, and creating; and even harder work justifying our spending (which I spent anyway). That we had to hire a dedicated resource teacher to lead in the design and implementation process was a big (and some would regard, unnecessary) expense as well.

Andrew (if you recall, he had been one of our first Baby Buddy clients) joined Wee Care as an investor and director in 2004. I had reached out to him a few months earlier because I was getting very worried about the way the school was going. I also knew that he had been an entrepreneur before and understood the challenges of running a small-medium enterprise. Plus, he was a banker by profession. To me, that meant he understood numbers far more than I did.

Andrew was adamant that school fees had to be raised and I felt that there was little choice by then but to do as he advised. The financial situation was really dire after all. The fallout from this fee increase, however, was sharp and rapid. We lost about a third of our families and for a while, things were very tense. To make matters worse, Andrew had to return to his old life in banking a few months after the fee hike; way before we could tell whether the financial restructuring would be successful or not. I felt quite alone when I was on my own again, deeply frightened that the whole endeavour would collapse like a house of cards.

Over and above the fear, I felt a terrible sense of guilt that I had subjected my poor husband to the stress (on top of his own work stress) of losing our investment in the business. He had been quietly shouldering the burden of my "adventure" (as he used to like calling it) from day one and had magnanimously not expected any contribution from me to our own family's finances for six, almost seven years by then. I felt terrible that I would be letting him down, and very sad at my own failure to solve the company's problems. In a nutshell, the persistent issue (to me anyway) seemed to boil down to an incompatibility between education and capitalism; either you gain the one and lose the other, or you gain the other and lose the one. It was like being caught, quite literally, between a rock and a hard place.

One day, very troubled, I decided to go off by myself to a quiet part of Singapore to think and pray.

No, let me be honest. I went off to cry ...

And cry and cry.

I cried my eyes out.

But I prayed too. I prayed and asked God if I had made the wrong decision to start Wee Care. I told Him that I had wanted to bless children, and that I thought it would work; how could it be that something that I thought would be a blessing was turning out to be a terrible mistake? Had I made the wrong assumptions? Had I heard wrong? That Wee Care was just a product of my own selfish ambitions? That underlying all of the blood and sweat and tears was just a shaky, wooden scaffold that was going to burn up like tinder very soon?

The questions that poured out of my heart were a confusing, tumbling mess of incoherent words and thoughts.

And then, out of nowhere—it was not a voice, it was more like a thought; but not a thought that popped into my head but a thought that plopped into my being; a short, simple sentence:

Look at the tree.

I stopped and looked around. Huh? Where had that come from? And what tree? Which tree? I was surrounded by trees.

The sentence was gentle but insistent.

Look at the tree.

I got up and started to walk.

Look at the tree.

What tree? Why tree? Is that you, God?

Look at the tree.

I stopped and looked at the nearest tree. And then, without warning, another soft, gentle sentence, almost imperceptible.

You planted a seed.

I gasped inwardly and took a sharp breath in. There and then, standing in the middle of nowhere, a million doubts suddenly washed away in a cascading shower of assurance and affirmation.

You planted a seed.

Yes.

Yes ...

Yes! I had planted a seed, and now, with all of the children we were serving, the school was very much like a tree. I had never really thought of it in those terms before. It was like the years suddenly compressed into a snapshot moment on account of those two simple and gentle sentences. I understood. I understood the reasons for the unanswered prayers and the years of stress and toil. I understood why it had taken so long and why there had been no financial reward up to that point.

I understood.

It had taken a very long time for the seed to sprout and grow, but Wee Care was now a tree. It had teachers for roots and parents pouring water and fertiliser into the ground; it had children like leaves, and sometimes, even though I did not want them to, the leaves would fall off with the passage of time; yet new ones would grow and, more than that ... the fruit would come.

The fruit will come.

The fruit will come.

I understood and now I knew. God had been there all along. God had been the master gardener giving my tree space to grow.[136] It was now a tree!

And the fruit will come.

The fruit will come? Dared I believe this?

I went home that evening a little tired, a little giddy, a little shocked, a little disbelieving; yet believing and comforted, excited and hopeful. Later that year, 2005, I would learn from our accountant and auditor that Wee Care had made a profit in the 2004 financial year. It was the first time we had done so since the company's founding. With the little money in my hand, I went and bought my husband a watch to say thank you. Andrew and I met over lunch too, where I was able to share the good news.

But more than anything, I was so grateful that God had brought life out of—in spite of—the wilderness; and that He had allowed me to be a gardener like Adam of old.

Trees are quite astonishing things, are they not? I have read that planet earth has more than 60,000 known species of trees.[137] From a single, mature, and leafy tree, enough oxygen for 2 to 10 people a year may be produced. At the same time, trees act as a valuable and natural check on excess carbon dioxide emissions. They help curb urban air pollution levels and counter the heat in cities. Trees also provide food, medicine, raw materials, shade/shelter, windbreaks, and flood control. Apparently, adding one tree to an open field can increase bird biodiversity from almost zero to as much as 80. Native trees create vital habitat for less obvious animals too, including squirrels, bats, and bees. Bees pollinate our plants and bats eat pests like mice and mosquitoes!

To me, thinking of Wee Care as a tree fundamentally changed my view of the company and the future. For one, I stopped grieving over the children who graduated or who had to leave the school. Even though my heart ached at times, I realised that it was natural for the school to experience cycles and seasons of "more students" or "fewer students". I started to look forward to new "branches" of growth, and I did not worry about some programmes not filling up once in a while. Instead, I realised that "pruning" might actually encourage growth in other areas. With one or two fewer programmes to worry about, the teachers, managers, and I could take stock of things, focus on improving our processes and protocols, as well as enhance the quality of our lessons and teaching methodologies.

Over and above these insights, a more important revelation came to me in the forthcoming months after that fateful day. I realised that new trees could and would grow from the **seeds** in the fruit. I began to ask myself what sorts of "seeds" the school had and how they could be sown to provide more food, medicine (e.g. therapy), and shelter (e.g. employment) to more children, families, and teachers. Was it our curriculum or teaching know-how? Was it the way the school was run as both a playschool, kindergarten, and early intervention centre?

I had many questions and not that many answers. But I dutifully started seeking advice and expertise.

The first place I reached out to—the Intellectual Property Office of Singapore (IPOS)—responded quickly and reassuringly to my query. They put Wee Care onto a scheme with an IPOS strategist as well as an external consultant to help me identify Wee Care's intellectual property (IP) and intangible assets (IA). The sessions I had with them were helpful and instructive. If I remember correctly, the amount I had to pay for these sessions was small compared to what I ultimately got back in knowledge and advice. It was also a small boost to my confidence to hear from the advisor and consultant that I had established a company that had **value**, not just in the financial sense but also in terms of its pedagogical competencies and business knowhow. While I would eventually still struggle with the tensions between education and capitalism, it helped to know that others recognised the heart and soul that I, an entrepreneur, had put into the business. Indeed, I deeply appreciated the Singapore government then for acknowledging what I had created, and what is more, for carving out resources that could and would extend my personal and professional goals for the school.

IPOS steered me into thinking about franchising as a possible avenue for business growth. I started communicating with a few consulting companies and eventually decided to work with Albert Kong and his team at Asiawide Franchise Consultants. Not only did Albert, Clarence, and Christine clarify many of the residual doubts I had about business growth (especially whether it would compromise the quality of Wee Care's programmes—it would not with the necessary safeguards), they also helped streamline my thinking about how growth should or could take place. For the first time in my life, I learnt what a financial model is, how to construct and read one, and how to use the numbers to frame business decisions. Both Clarence and Christine helped me put together our first ever Franchise Manual, which gave both the broad strokes and finer details of how a Wee Care school should operate. They also helped Wee Care secure a grant from Enterprise Singapore (formerly International Enterprise Singapore and SPRING Singapore) to offset their consulting fees!

It was an exciting time to say the least. I was overjoyed to note the baby steps we were taking towards "sowing" our seeds further afield. With counsel from Yew Woon Chooi, a leading franchise lawyer and intellectual property practitioner recommended by the Asiawide team, I extended the franchising programme to include a licensing programme, the latter to formally train up Home Buddies to undertake employment as semi-autonomous home-therapy "contractors". This programme did surprisingly well. We were very selective about who we trained, and the therapeutic results of their rehabilitation efforts were notable. Families tended to stay with these Home Buddies for years.

The process of franchising and licensing also made me realise it would be viable to start another company-owned early intervention centre in Singapore. Up to the late 2000s, Wee Care was still one of the few centres in Singapore providing behavioural and educational therapy for young children with special needs. We urgently needed the capacity to take in more students. Their needs were pressing as many of them had few resources, specialists, and/or programmes to turn to. Most of the special schools were filled and had long waiting lists.

In the middle of 2008, Wee Care at Everton Park opened. The unit was very close to Chinatown and on the ground floor of an HDB block. It jostled for presence and visibility amongst maid agencies, sundry shops, a pet grooming studio, printing companies as well as one or two hipster cafes and a few units promoting traditional Chinese medicine (TCM). I liked that there was a large food court behind our new centre—a convenient place for the team and I to go get lunch! We celebrated the opening with an Open Day filled with games, bubbles, and balloons. An elderly family friend came by with two of her young twin granddaughters. They had a great time jumping up and down, trying to catch the balloons that were floating about the centre. My very own Baby 3 was there too. I had given birth to her in 2006.

Baby 3 had been a slightly more demanding pregnancy to carry. I was significantly older when pregnant with her than when I had had

Babies 1 and 2. Nausea accompanied me throughout the nine months and a bad backache during the last trimester. Plus, I put on a lot of weight! My obstetrician said that I should test for abnormalities in the foetus because I was now in the "high-risk" category but I refused. It was not an easy thought and I got stressed thinking about the possible scenarios that might come up. But I knew that I would not be able to raise my hand against Baby 3 and terminate the pregnancy even if the final prognosis was not good. I figured that if God had decided to give us a special child, I would have to put considerable action to my words and love her unconditionally nonetheless. I also knew that together with her two older sisters, Baby 3 would complete our family and, indeed, she did.

The new early intervention centre provided a special preschool programme in the mornings that I termed "First Starts". It was meant to be a bridging programme before the child's eventual inclusion into a regular preschool. In the afternoons, we continued with individual sessions of behaviour therapy either at the centre or for some children, within their homes. On Saturdays, the extra rooms afforded us the space to expand our social skills playgroup programme. Our therapists were indeed kept very busy. More importantly, an excellent senior therapist joined us who helped me manage the centre with care and professionalism. I am not sure what I would have done without her. Within two years, we broke even. It was a heart-warming confirmation of all that I had heard that day in the park.

More importantly, the growth that the early intervention centre was showing assured me that our financial model was sound. It also assured potential franchisees that Wee Care was a worthwhile endeavour to invest in. Quite coincidentally, around the time our preparation for franchising concluded, a former teacher—a young

Indonesian lady called Luci whom I admired and respected for her diligence and work ethic—indicated that she was ready to, indeed wanted to, start a Wee Care centre in Jakarta, Indonesia.

Luci and I had talked a lot before she returned to Jakarta to get married and start a family. She had come to Singapore at the young age of 24, secured permanent residency, and worked her way up from preschool teacher to vice principal at Wee Care within two years. Luci was dynamic, earnest, and honest. She jumped and sang with enthusiasm. She taught with passion and fortitude. In the playground, she was a superhero. She would catch children from falling or from slamming into things by accident. One Singaporean mother told me how awed she was by Luci's energy. Once, she put a few children in separate IKEA roller crates that had been tied together in a long line like a train. Singing at the top of her lungs, she single-handedly pushed and pulled the children along an imaginary train.

It was obvious to me that Luci's heart was in the right place. She had told me more than once that Indonesian children would benefit immensely from the play-based methodologies used by Wee Care. She also knew that many children with special needs were not being served in her homeland. In this, what she found the most inspiring was that Wee Care had a model of early childhood education and early intervention/therapy that was "under one roof". Moreover, now that she had seen it, been part of it, and learnt from it, she knew that it could be done; and she wanted it for Indonesian children and families too. Listening to Luci was like listening to my younger self; imagining her future reality was like seeing the world though rose-tinted glasses again. Like me, Luci wanted "life" to emerge in a stretch of wilderness too; but in a different place, one that she had grown up in and was familiar with.

In all of our interactions, I think it helped that Luci and I shared a common heritage. My paternal great-grandmother had been Sundanese and I had spent many happy holidays as a child in Indonesia, immersed in the culture and language of an indulgent posse of grandparents, aunts, and uncles. The thought that Wee Care might start a centre in Jakarta, albeit a licensed one, thrilled me to bits. But more than that, the thought that this would constitute another planted seed, one that would grow into another symbolic tree for food, medicine, and shelter, was exhilarating.

I flew to Jakarta for the launch day in September 2008. Luci and her business partners had worked hard preparing a large two-storey house in the north of the capital. Based on my estimates, the centre at full capacity would be able to serve 220 children a day (in three shifts) and this before accounting for the children attending early intervention sessions. Not only were there were many rooms in the house, there were also many willing hands eager for work. I really enjoyed getting to know the new team, and training them. I enjoyed meeting Indonesian parents too, listening to their concerns and learning that they were no different from parents in Singapore and around the world. While it was not always easy transferring (and at times, transmuting) the concepts of education and therapy into forms that could be assimilated into and/or accommodated by the Indonesian worldview, I learnt a lot in the process—not just about the "other" but about myself too, and about the way knowledge is very often the product of a mutual co-construction between two parties.

By the time Wee Care Singapore was sold in late 2017, Wee Care Jakarta had matured enough to separate amicably from the parent company. It took on a new name, logo, and image. It also moved into an even larger house in an adjoining neighbourhood. Luci and I still talk on the phone occasionally, and I have flown over to visit her and to observe how her "new" school is progressing. It touches me whenever I notice that many of the same pedagogical principles and corporate values that characterised Wee Care are still an essential part of life in her centre. But it touches me more to know that the preschool is still giving life and seeding life for the benefit of many more children, families, and staff. I could not have known, so many years before, that one seed would be able to do so much.

A year later, in 2009, one of our father-clients at the main Wee Care centre collaborated with two business partners, Vanessa and I'Ling, to start our fourth Wee Care school (our third in Singapore) along the east coast of Singapore. Hariman's vision was to entwine the preschool with his indoor playground business, The Polliwogs. It was ingenious, mutually beneficial, and also developmentally enriching. Wee Care students could take advantage of the indoor playground during their regular break times. They could also come back on the weekends to play or to celebrate their birthdays in one of the tastefully-decorated party rooms that ran along one side of the facility. Hariman devised amazing activities for his and our clients, including having a massive bouncy inflatable, an enormous slide, just outside the centre. The children loved climbing up and sliding down! They loved the intricacies of the play-gym too, which included platforms and ball pits, all padded and sanitised regularly. I loved that the children were developing their skills in spatial awareness, eye-hand coordination, and gross-motor abilities in the process.

This partnership was an effective one because Vanessa and Hariman both had strong backgrounds in business and finance, plus Vanessa had also already obtained a qualification in early childhood education prior to our exploratory conversations. I'Ling had practised as a therapist at a well-known autism centre prior to the venture. She was ready to lead her own team of therapists at Wee Care Polliwogs. I was amazed at the way this group of investors had come together; it seemed so natural and yet it could only have been divinely ordained. Each of their three backgrounds exemplified the mission and purpose for Wee Care like a braided rope. Collectively, another seed was thus also planted and I could look forward to the future with a sense of hope and wonder.

We sang this song at Wee Care very often. It was fun but also a challenge to remember! To me, the song encapsulates the themes of this chapter, that life begets life, and how joy emerges from that. Do sing along with me if you know the melody.

>Oh in the woods, there was a tree
>The prettiest tree
>That you ever did see
>And the tree was in the hole
>And the hole was in the ground
>And the green grass grew all around, all around,
>and the green grass grew all around.
>
>And on that tree, there was a limb
>The prettiest limb
>That you ever did see
>And the limb was on the tree
>And the tree in the hole

And the hole was in the ground
And the green grass grew all around, all around,
And the green grass grew all around.

And on that limb, there was a branch
The prettiest branch
That you ever did see
And the branch was on the limb,
And the limb was on the tree,
And the tree was in the hole
And the hole was in the ground
And the green grass grew all around, all around,
And the green grass grew all around.

And on that branch, there was a nest
The prettiest nest
That you ever did see
And the nest was on the branch
And the branch was on the limb
And the limb was on the tree
And the tree was in the hole
And the hole was in the ground
And the green grass grew all around, all around,
And the green grass grew all around.

And in that nest, there was an egg
The prettiest egg
That you ever did see
And the egg was in the nest

And the nest was on the branch
And the branch was on the limb
And the limb was on the tree
And the tree was in the hole
And the hole was in the ground
And the green grass grew all around, all around,
And the green grass grew all around.

And in that egg, there was a bird
The prettiest bird
That you ever did see
And the bird was in the egg
And the egg was in the nest
And the nest was on the branch
And the branch was on the limb
And the limb was on the tree
And the tree was in the hole
And the hole was in the
And the green grass grew all around, all around,
And the green grass grew all around.

---

136 Genesis 2:8; John 15:1. *The Holy Bible* (NIV version).
137 McLendon, R. (2020, January 14). *15 astounding facts about trees.* Treehugger: Sustainability for All. https://www.treehugger.com/facts-about-trees-4868798

11

SHARING FRUIT

Around the time Wee Care was seeding new schools in Singapore and Jakarta, an opportunity arose for us to "sow" further afield in a non-profit capacity. A very good friend of mine, Sarah, had moved to North India in the early 2000s to establish a village preschool in the Himalayan foothills, in what was formerly the state of Uttaranchal. Sarah had not pressured me to visit, but I was curious to know how she was and what life in India was like. The thought of a working holiday was very far from my mind, to be honest. Instead, I was keen on a mental break and India seemed like a unique destination, far-off, exotic, and mysterious.

Unbeknownst to me then, that first visit to India would end up seeding life in two ways, one existential and the other practical. First and foremost, it seeded a new and far bigger vision in my heart that effective educational outreach to children, families, and teachers in more impoverished or disadvantaged backgrounds was not only possible, but extremely needful and important. Second, it laid the groundwork for the tone and structure of subsequent teaching/training missions to India (and elsewhere) that many Wee Care staff would also choose to participate in on a completely voluntary basis. Between 2005 to 2018, these—our "corporate social responsibility" (or CSR)—trips took place at least once a year.

In another sense, though, there were no two ways about it. I fell in love with India that first trip. Not that I did not see the problems that are prevalent in India. There are problems in India that frighten me tremendously. But India is more than its problems. India is its people.

It helped that Luci and Joyce (one of Wee Care's early behaviour therapists) had agreed to accompany me. They were probably curious about India too; or worried I might not return to Singapore safely! It helped even more that a lovely Wee Care mother, Viji, had very kindly offered to have us stay over at her in-law's home in New Delhi upon arrival. We landed near midnight and I remember thinking I would have been completely lost and overwhelmed had I been required to find my way around the confusion on my own. There was such a commotion in the arrival hall, and so much activity. Overeager employees were pushing hotel name plaques into our faces at every turn. At the airport exit, drivers of auto-rickshaws rushed forward without a care, invading our personal spaces and shouting offers to drive us wherever we wanted to go.

Thankfully, Viji's parents-in-law had arranged a private chauffeur to pick us up from the airport. Later, I found out that this gentleman would also be driving us the next day from Delhi to Dehradun (a journey of some 250 kilometres) along some very exciting, even dangerous, roads. At one stretch, we were accosted by the sight of an overturned lorry. It had been overladen with bales and bales of straw of some kind, piled so high that it must have toppled over with just a minor miscalculated turn of its frame. At another stretch, we found ourselves inching through a massive traffic jam. The traffic lights had gone out and an unending stream of vehicles from the north, south, east, and west were converging at the junction with reckless abandonment. No one wanted to give each other way. It was taking one brave policeman with a wooden stick to bring some order to the chaos, and even then, with very little success. We managed to get out of the scrum about an hour later.

But I loved it, and no one was more surprised than me. I loved the energy and the incessant sounds; the bright, dichotomous colours that leapt from the greyness and brownness of the dusty buildings and countryside; the unexpected strangeness of it all, like when a cow decided to sit in the middle of the road and drivers began pleading with it to move, or when pigs suddenly appeared next to the car like automobiles of a different kind.

I loved it more when we neared Dehradun and the mountains came into sight. They were breathtaking.

Do these belong to the Himalaya, I wondered?

We drove for hours and hours, past winding forested roads and then the busy city of Dehradun, down a tree-lined avenue, and then a small road that seemed to go higher and higher into the hills. Sarah and I had managed a quick international call—these were the days before WhatsApp and Messenger—where I had asked her where she was and hmmm ... where were we?

Stop there. I'm coming on the scooter. You must have driven past me. The Creative Learning Centre is along the road you're on.

Ah, the preschool! We had arrived safely.

I took in the three rooms and the children's art on the walls with genuine interest. I peeked into the kitchen and breathed in the new smells. I stared at the picturesque landscape of trees, hills, and fields beyond the verandah. Tiny houses dotted the rustic topography, sharp contrasts to the soaring steel and glass edifices of Singapore.

There was human life in these homes, evidenced by the pockets of light that were bursting through the small windows in the descending darkness of the evening. I was very glad to be there, tired but safe. My bed that night, though narrow and hard, was a grateful respite.

But it was the children, the next day, who made up for all the discomforts we had endured. They were a mix of Indian, Tibetan, and Nepali children; beautiful, calm, and well-behaved. Luci could not help but notice how generous they were with the food treats we had brought along.

"In Singapore," she said, "they would be fighting over the Oreos already. Look, they are giving each other a biscuit before taking one themselves."

Indeed, the children were kind, unassuming, curious, and happy. Their teachers, on the other hand, were determined, motivated, and eager to learn.

"Teach us how to teach better," was the consistent refrain.

And so, I did. I taught on domains of development and shared ideas on the kinds of playful tasks they could engage in that would best meet objectives in early childhood development and education. The next day, we demonstrated music and movement activities with scarves cut from translucent fabric, as well as maracas and streamers made from recycled materials. We hip-hopped, then swayed to a slow song. We took the children on our laps for action songs. There was a lot of squealing and laughing.

> Down by the banks of the hanky-panky,
> Where the bullfrogs jump from bank to bank-y,
> With an oops ... oops ... belly-flop.
> One missed the lily-pad and went ker-plop!

Amidst all of these happy interactions, we were occasionally interrupted by ... wild monkeys—rhesus macaques! I had seen them along the roads when travelling but had not anticipated how daring and clever they were. At the second training session, one female monkey, baby clinging to her tummy, entered the kitchen while we were in the classroom, probably to get her hands on some of our tea biscuits. It was quite a scene when all of the teachers got up to give chase, one with a long stick. I remember Sarah calling out, "Be careful, they are dangerous" which made me fall behind the group. I could teach and train for sure, but not monkeys!

Another time, a monkey tried to come through the front door of the preschool. I yelped, the anxious city girl. One Indian teacher stood up, sari and all, and grabbed the closest thing she could find to throw in the direction of the fleeing animal. It turned out to be my chappal, my slipper. I saw it fly a good 50 metres over a boundary wall and land in a plot of uninhabited land next door. I gasped and looked at the teacher with wide eyes.

"It is one of the only pair of shoes I have here."

"Don't worry, Ma'am," she said with an assuring Indian shake of her head, "I will get it back for you."

True enough, before I knew it, she had asked a village boy to scale the wall. He returned grinning, slipper in hand. His smile widened when the teacher gave him a handful of small rupees in exchange.

"Those monkeys are a terrible nuisance," Sarah told me repeatedly. "One time, we found a baby monkey in the kitchen. It had come in through a tiny space in the window grille and was passing food—our food—to its family members outside!"

The challenges to running the preschool were real and all I wanted to do at times was to give my friend a hug. In addition to issues related to teaching quality and the financial sustainability of the school, Sarah was also grappling with water and electricity cuts, monkey problems, health, hygiene and safety concerns as well as cultural (mindset) differences on a daily basis. It was a tough, tough undertaking, which inevitably strengthened my resolve to do as much as I could to train, inspire, and encourage her, and her teachers, as much as possible.

A quick drive and walk along the road the second afternoon of our visit had yielded treasures from the village shops: colourful plastic jugs and one or two kilos of daal which we used for a lesson on pouring. This was my suggested substitute for writing, equally effective if not more appropriate for two- to four-year-olds learning to coordinate their hands and eyes. The children were completely enthralled. For the first time, they were getting edgy and spontaneous, all eager for a turn at the table to attempt the task, on their own, without spilling.

We played with play dough next, improvising a dramatic skit where I made "cookies" to share out, but making counting errors once in a while to instigate thoughtful reactions that would reinforce the children's understanding of cardinality. The children were thrilled to be able to correct me; this democratic space—created deliberately and guarded zealously by those who advocate for children's rights—was something that they had probably never experienced before.

It is possible—no, it is good—for children to have "the right to freedom of expression". When they are enabled to "seek, receive, and impart information and ideas of all kinds" and in whatever form they wish (including spoken, written, art, or any kind of media),[138] education is profoundly humanised. In this kind of education, there is a participatory construction of knowledge where the adults, children, and the community are in relationship with one another. The children get to experience their world through communication, participation, information exchange, and cooperation. Schools are merely spaces—complex and living ecosystems, I would add—for relationship and socialisation.[139]

Our last day was spent showing the teachers how to weave drama and puppet play into their lessons. We encouraged them, and the children, to take turns dressing up and enacting character roles in "Little Red Riding Hood". The enthusiasm in the room was joyful, infectious, and palpable. But my attention was on a different drama; the one speaking to me that the little investment of time and effort that I had put into the trip was already yielding so much in return and so quickly, its impact on a multiplicity of lives immediately evident. This was, to me, capacity-building at its most meaningful and profound.

Indeed, it did not seem untenable to me at all—huddled in that small blue village classroom, each of us a little speck of life and movement against the stolid majesty of the Himalayas—that emotional, relational, and longer-term cognitive and creative "fruit" would emerge from the very small seeds I was sowing.

Heart-pumping, life-giving, sacred;
this education
that values
you, me, he, she, they.
Will you walk and talk with us too?
Take my hand.

Flying back to Singapore though, I found myself fighting logic and reality. How much could we help ... really? After all, the Wee Care teachers and I could, at the very most, visit North India once or twice a year only. Plus, the demands of our work lives were exhausting enough. The first day of the new term, I felt like a kitchen towel thrown into a washing machine again, whirled and tossed about in an unending cycle of routines, schedules, sounds, and activities.

Preschool noises—
these interruptions of
teacher talking, calling, persuading, chiding, telling, and
children crying, complaining,
now laughing, giggling—

Shoes, bags, bottles, books
shoved, dropped,
shuffled, dragged.

Bang, goes the door
of the classroom
where muffled voices hum for half-an-hour before

Creak, goes the door again
and excited voices
fill the corridor
of my mind—
this labyrinth—
thinking
of other children
far, far away.

It was not long after, perhaps a week or two later, that I chanced to read an excerpt of scripture during my usual morning devotion.

"I will make rivers flow on barren heights,
and springs within the valleys.
I will turn the desert into pools of water,
and the parched ground into springs.

I will put in the desert the cedar and the acacia,
the myrtle and the olive.
I will set pines in the wasteland,
the fir and the cypress together."[140]

I stopped and reread the verses. Strange—I had never noticed them before. The references to trees—specific trees—were uncanny but not in a disturbing way.

Is that you again, God?
What are you saying?

I thought about the scripture verses whenever my mind strayed back to India. In context, I knew that they were referring to God making a promise through the prophet Isaiah to bring life to an austere, inhospitable land. But it seemed that there was a link now, a link between these other trees and Wee Care.

In the weeks after, whenever time permitted, I looked up whatever information I could find about the listed trees. It seemed to me, after research and reflection, that each of the trees represented a different value of particular significance. The myrtle, for instance, appeared to be representative of "healing". Its leaves, fruit, and flowers have been used, after all, for medicinal purposes since ancient times. Moreover, not only does the plant have anti-hyperglycaemic, analgesic, antigenotoxic, and antibacterial properties, parts of the plant can be used for food and in cosmetics.[141] Similarly, the olive tree seemed to me symbolic of "sustenance". As most of us know, it has been cultivated for centuries and is of major agricultural importance to the Mediterranean region as a source of oil and food.[142] The oil, I have learnt, is composed of predominantly monounsaturated fatty acids.[143] These are healthier than saturated fats!

I could not decide what kind of a tree Wee Care was. But I did surmise that there is incalculable value to all kinds of trees, all kinds of plants. Life would not be life as we know it without the wood of the teak for our furniture, the husk of the coconut for doormats, brushes, ropes and strings, and the fruit from the lime, mango, papaya, rambutan, and guava—just to name a few—for our South East Asian palates.

In the same way, there is value to all kinds of businesses and work efforts so that—as I began exploring this astonishing idea in my mind tentatively—there must be all sorts of possible and multiple ways for Wee

Care and/or I to seed life in India ... and elsewhere? It need not be strictly in the areas of early childhood education or early intervention solely.

Slowly and gradually, with this assumption at the back of my mind, I began to look into ideas for different projects that could be undertaken for the benefit of the children, women, and families of the village. To their amazing credit, Sarah and her colleagues were completely gracious and supportive. They went out of their way to do whatever they could, especially before any of our visits, to promote, facilitate, and encourage our efforts.

Once, I conducted a hands-on, experiential workshop on "running your own small business". It was attended by about a dozen ladies from the women's training centre located about 100 metres up the hill from the preschool. In the session, I asked the participants to craft a business idea, then promote and sell their imagined products or services to as many people as possible. Some of the male employees in the training centre were roped in as pretend customers!

In the session, I handed out mah-jong chips that I had purchased from Chinatown in Singapore and told the ladies that their goal was to accumulate as many of these chips as possible (their "revenue") but that I would collect two chips every ten minutes for "rent" and one chip every twenty minutes for "advertising". It was hilarious yet gratifying to watch the energy and activity that ensued from these instructions. The women made signs and welcomed "customers" who had each been given their own individual purse of mah-jong chips for spending. The "entrepreneurs" came up with fresh ideas for new and interesting products and services—some with a novel twist; there was good teamwork and communication at every table.

Another time, we ran a Health Camp for the students of a slum school that two of Sarah's colleagues had planted in the nearby city of

Dehradun. It started with a preliminary health check of the children's weight, height, and common ailments, followed by lessons about nutrition and self-care. We showed the children how to make their own egg sandwiches (explaining along the way why a simple meal like this would be considered nutritious) before rotating them in small groups across a variety of stations for games and easy physical exercises. We taught them how to brush their teeth too; although I have to confess I ended up thoroughly regretting this aspect of the day. To introduce the topic, we had scripted a drama performance that, quite unfortunately, backfired completely. One of the younger primary students took fright at my persona as "bacteria". Thinking that it would make me look funny, I had donned a pink wig and jumped out from behind a tree growling and howling. The poor child was not impressed. He screamed so loudly and with such terror that I thought he might pass out.

The Health Camp fortuitously opened a means for us to communicate with the children's mothers afterwards. This debrief session was a complete eye-opener to me. In spite of the gut-wrenching deprivation and oppression that these women were in, in spite of their marginalised status, they were like any other mother anywhere in the world. They crowded around asking and seeking solutions to their individual child's health issues. They were interested to know, eager to find out, not hapless or helpless. They were motivated to keep their progeny alive and to maximise their chances for success, however miserably constrained their culture had prescribed their lives to be.

Once a mother, always a mother.

It would probably take too long for me to describe the rest of the initiatives Wee Care was privileged to be a part of in India. But recalling them quickly, I think of the educational conference we spoke at (that incorporated topics on special needs' education), regular in-service training sessions for the teachers of the preschool and slum school, visits to colleagues' pioneering schools higher up in the mountains, and even self-defence classes for youth and women. I would not be exaggerating when I say that the memories of these extraordinary experiences will have a special place in my heart forever.

But these experiences were significant for another reason. Because of our "successes" in India, I slowly developed the confidence to launch Wee Care into other CSR projects, even if they fell outside of our usual ambit. In 2012, a number of Wee Care teachers and I put up our first ever fundraising event using storytelling and song as a platform for generating ticket sales. In all, we put up a total of five fundraisers—each one held in Wee Care's rooftop garden—amassing thousands of dollars each time for charities across Asia, including child-focused ones in Malaysia, Cambodia, Timor Leste, and our very own Care Corner in Singapore. In this, I was particularly happy when Care Corner allowed their students to come and watch the performances themselves. We had the children bussed over on a weekday afternoon just before or after the scheduled weekend shows. It was such a joy to see them laughing and singing along each time. In 2017, we took our show to North India too—quite a logistics feat!—performing for both the preschool families and the students from the slum school.

Then, in 2018, I received an email. It was from a medical doctor in Singapore who asked if I would be willing to help the first autism-specific school in Phnom Penh, Cambodia, improve the quality of their therapy and educational programmes. I replied to say that, of course, I would be willing. One visit became two visits and have now progressed to ongoing Zoom seminars where I have been able to train the teachers and parents on a range of issues, including how to respond to behaviour problems and overcome communication difficulties.

This is not to say that Wee Care was neglected during the many years we were reaching out to support non-profit and charity organisations around Asia. In addition to planting more Wee Care schools, we were also simultaneously extending the range of our local programmes by pushing out more "branches" within each of our centres. These included enrichment sessions in the afternoons that focused not on academic-style learning but more imaginative subjects such as Mandarin speech and drama, creative art, creative movement, and creative writing. They were surprisingly popular and helped shore up our revenue line, which we had to keep growing in order to cope with annual inflations in salaries and rent.

But the bottom line for me was this really: None of our giving would have been possible without the resources made possible by our main Wee Care school. I would not have been able to do what I did without competent staff holding the fort whenever I was out of the country. Our trips and fundraising efforts would have been pitiful had they not included the input of many of Wee Care's highly talented teachers and therapists. The people who paid for and attended our fundraisers were our hugely supportive parents and their children. In addition, funds for flights, training materials, and props would not have been possible without profits and the computers and other (cutting, printing, laminating, binding) machines already available within our various centres.

I have thus learnt this thing about capitalism. You can do two things with money: Keep everything for yourself, or share what you have, in whichever way you can and with those who would most benefit from it, like a large basket of delectable fruit. After all, fruit will spoil when it is left out for too long without being eaten.

---

138 United Nations General Assembly (1989, November 20). *Convention on the Rights of the Child*. United Nations Human Rights, Office of the High Commissioner. https://www.ohchr.org/en/professionalinterest/pages/crc.aspx
139 Sousa, D. (2020). Towards a democratic ECEC system. In C. Cameron & P. Moss (Eds.), *Transforming early childhood in England: Towards a democratic education* (pp. 151–169). London: UCL Press.
140 Isaiah 41:18–19. *The Holy Bible* (NIV version).
141 Amensour, M., Sendra, E., Abrini, J., Bouhdid, S., Perez-Alvarez, J. A., & Fernandez-Lopez, J. (2009). Total phenolic content and antioxidant activity of myrtle (myrtus communis) extracts. *Natural Product Communications, 4*(6), 819–824. https://journals.sagepub.com/doi/pdf/10.1177/1934578X0900400616
142 Vossen, P. (2007). Olive oil: history, production, and characteristics of the world's classic oils. *American Society for Horticultural Science, 42*(5), pp.1093–1100.
143 Riley, F. R. (2002). Olive oil production on bronze age Crete: Nutritional properties, processing methods, and storage life of Minoan olive oil. *Oxford Journal of Archaeology, 21*(1), 63–75.

12

GROWING UP, GROWING OLD

I cannot remember when exactly it happened but I remember the sensory details of the moment like yesterday. I had gone into the Open Learning playroom to check on someone or something, maybe to turn the volume down on the music player or to ascertain if the lesson was going well. As would often happen in the midst of a dozen two- and three-year-olds, I stopped to talk to a child, an interaction that—as far as I was concerned, anyway—would necessitate a bit of play. Without much thought, I dropped to my knees so that my face would be at the child's eye-level.

And then, the pain.

Not the pain of, say, a bump or a bruise, mind you, but sharp, shooting pains that radiated all the way up my left leg through to my spine and brain. Pain unlike pain I had ever felt before because it was intense and unrelenting; crippling, to say the least. I could only gasp and hold still in response. To an external observer, I was probably just lost in thought. Indeed, no one in the playroom, not a single teacher, seemed to notice anything amiss. But a more attentive onlooker would have seen the shock and wince on my face. The pain lasted, in all probability, for less than a minute but it felt like a very long time. I could not move, talk, or think straight until the agony subsided.

What just happened there?

I mustered a weak smile for the child I had been intending to speak with and redirected him (or was it her?) to another activity. Once discharged of this responsibility, I rose hesitatingly to my feet and walked back to my office. It was strange. I expected to stagger or limp, but I could walk normally. To avoid quizzical stares or questions from well-meaning staff, I resisted the urge to tug my trouser leg up to have a good look at my knee.

That night, I sat and stared down. What had caused the pain? I expected a bruise where I had felt the anguish but there was nothing to show for the discomfort I had endured. It was all the more puzzling because there had been a thick rubber mat where I had knelt. Plus, what I had done was a movement so habitual and rehearsed that I could not possibly have pulled a muscle in the process.

There was nothing different about my knee, only a small bony bump just below the knee joint that I had never noticed before. How could that have caused the pain and what was it anyway? It felt like bone. It did not feel like a tumour, not that I knew what tumours felt like.

A quick Google search revealed that the bump was probably a bone spur, a symptom of possible osteoarthritis or a natural outcome of ageing: wear and tear! Apparently, bone spurs arise when the body attempts to repair itself.

"Hmmph," I thought, quite unimpressed that that was all it was, and quite incredulous too that a minor impact against a bone spur could cause so much pain. At the same time, I could not help but reflect, in the days afterward, on my advancing age and how all of the parents and teachers at Wee Care did not seem to mind or even notice who or what I was becoming. Not that I was **old** and not that I wanted to be a victim, not at all, of ageism. Indeed, I did not fancy the idea of being bluntly written off as irrelevant or incapable. In my mind, I still had a great deal to contribute to early childhood education and early intervention. I still had hopes, dreams, and aspirations, both personal, professional, and for Wee Care.

But the feeling was there and I had to face it; that awful sense of not being cared for, of being overlooked as a human being with feelings and needs. The years of slogging and serving had become a normal part of my life but there were occasions—and these were occurring more and more often—when I wondered whether all of the sacrifices I had made for Wee Care (and by this, I mean the children, their families, and teachers) had been worth it. I was nowhere close to being a wealthy woman, not like some educational entrepreneurs who had grown their brands through mergers, takeovers, or aggressive franchising, or who had cleverly maximised their profits through larger class sizes and/or high fees. In contrast, in spite of its many years, Wee Care was still a struggling endeavour because of my unpragmatic ideals: that of being a caring and inclusive environment built on an ethos of equality, warmth, and love. Where we could, we were giving subsidies and discounts on the quiet to help families who needed the assistance. We were providing field trips and tickets to our annual concert for free. I was still working 50 to 60 hours per week— full days on Saturdays—to maintain my insane (administrative, clinical, pedagogical, leadership) schedule—and this after delegating what I could! It was not difficult to feel grossly unappreciated at times.

But it was not growing older per se that accentuated these feelings. In fact, growing older made me feel a little wiser and more circumspect. It was, however, making me wonder about the future more and more. The demands of running the school were unrelenting and would never let up, or so it seemed. And my body was telling me something else. That it would give, at some point, whether I wanted it to or not. It was not like I was sick or anything. I was still strong, active, and healthy. But growing and feeling older was real.

Another incident about a year later highlighted the approaching force of this reality in a slightly different way. Like the first though, it took me completely by surprise and for a while, I found it hard to understand (or accept, perhaps) the way my "new" body was acting.

I had, as much as possible, always tried to be present during field trips with the teachers and children. It was not a desire for control as much as it was a genuine concern for the safety and well-being of all of the participants. Unlike other preschools that tended to take their children out in small groups of, say, just the Kindergarten 1 and/or Kindergarten 2 classes, most field trips at Wee Care were massive exercises comprising up to 100 or 120 adults and students each time. Yes, there would be up to three big tour buses (or four medium-sized school buses) involved!

The reason our outings were this size was because every learning group at Wee Care shared a component called Life Skills which we conducted every Wednesday; and how and where could Life Skills best be learnt but in the natural settings of life? We visited parks and reservoirs, commercial kitchens and bakeries, museums and offices, the airport, and the zoo/bird park. Once, we even boarded a ferry to St John's Island and saw dolphins frolicking in Singapore waters on the way back to the mainland! It was all very exciting. But the process of planning and undertaking each adventure was exceedingly time-consuming and labour-intensive.

I will be the first to admit that I enjoyed these trips because they were a good excuse to get out of the office into nature. But there were historical and pragmatic reasons too. For one, I had led outings in the pioneering years and the staff seemed to assume that I should continue to do so; although I did insist eventually that the teachers should manage smaller field trips on their own. The second reason was to increase safety for the children. Because up to half of each outing was made up of two- and three-year-old students (we generally maintained a ratio of one teacher to two or three of these students for the duration of each outing), my availability meant that we could maintain that ratio effectively and/or allow for "eyes in front and at the back" whenever these were needed. To describe this another way, I would lead in the front to show the group where to go but I could also run to the back to ensure that no one had veered off, gotten lost, or been left behind in a toilet somewhere.

This necessitated a great deal of walking and running, of course. But it was all part of the fun of each day, and I would be gratified to observe the children's and teachers' enjoyment whenever a trip went well and things were learnt. Sometimes, parents, grandparents, and/or nannies would ask to come along too, which made the outing an intense social event. Not that I minded (we always tried to accommodate requests) but it could all be pretty exhausting at times!

In the early years, exhaustion was just a feeling to tolerate. I reasoned that I would be able to sleep it off the same night. Hence, it became a practice for me that after every outing, I would endeavour to push on and continue working. This meant that I would dismiss the teachers and students at noon, rush home for a quick shower and lunch, before returning to my office at Wee Care by 2:30 that same afternoon. Rushing like this, I would be able to put in another three to four hours of productive work before dinner—answering emails, reading lesson plans or Individual Educational Plans (IEPs), and/or checking in on special needs' students who were in session with their respective therapists that afternoon.

I did this for years, until one particular afternoon around 2012 or 2013. After arriving home from the field trip, I promptly fell asleep, something that I had never done before. I am not sure how long I slept for (maybe 15 to 20 minutes) but I remember being really puzzled at my drowsiness, then thoroughly shocked at myself when I woke up.

Surely not? I was not sick.

But tired from a field trip? How was that possible? I was invincible … supposedly. The lady who had gone back to work three days after giving birth to Babies 2 and 3. The woman who had not taken any "confinement", who had refused traditional tonics and soups, and who had nursed her children till they were two-year-olds. *Tired?!*

But tired I was, and yet, it seemed like I had no choice but to keep going. Somehow, being tired and/or feeling older was not within the permissible discourse for "successful" women in Singapore.

Or for anybody, for that matter.

In 2019, a commentary on Channel NewsAsia (CNA) confirmed that older workers in Singapore are often looked upon unfavourably.[144] Caustic attitudes might express themselves in online comments such as, "no company will employ older workers except in security and cleaning" and "older workers are obsolete". Indeed, the article underscored that older workers are perceived as "contributing less than their fair share and are not worth the extra money compared to younger workers".

To a certain extent, we have only ourselves as a society to blame for these beliefs. When I was growing up and in primary school, images of old people in stimulus pictures for Mandarin composition writing were always that of a white-haired woman (with her hair in a bun) needing help with a basket of vegetables, or that of a bent, elderly man with a walking stick needing assistance to cross a road. I was taught to use words such as "slow" and "needy" to describe them, and that I was "responsible" and "respectful" for helping them. As described forcefully in the CNA paper, associating old age with disease and disability have "reinforced the notion that life after 60 can only go downhill".

It is understandable when an older person chooses to resist this stereotyping. Indeed, after my sleep-in, I promptly brushed it aside as a one-time thing and threw myself back into work with a vengeance. It is only now, almost a decade later, that I realise my body was speaking to me, telling me of the changes happening inside, the symptoms of an approaching transition into midlife that could not be avoided; a transition that I needed to learn to manage, accompanied by the first lesson to care for myself with gentleness and acceptance.

Research studies tell us that what happens in the personal lives of teachers significantly affects the realisation of their professional roles.[145] While I had decided to ignore my maturing body, an older teacher at Wee Care had not. A dear and hard-working lady with years of experience in the field, she worked at Wee Care around the same time I was experiencing these changes. One day, she came and told me that she had been to KK Hospital for disturbing symptoms brought on by menopause. She was so shaken and upset that she felt she had no choice but to resign from her position. I asked her why she could not stay as we would be willing to give her time off to recuperate. It was the medical expenses, she explained. She was not a citizen or permanent resident and could not possibly afford to get medical care in Singapore.

Reflecting further, I wondered whether it was also the nature of early years' teaching that makes staying on as an older teacher more difficult. After all, preschoolers are high-energy creatures who need constant care and supervision. It takes strong knees to jump and dance, strong arms to lift a crying child, even stronger limbs and a healthy heart to clean out the sandpit, and/or empty the inflatable pools. It takes mental alertness as well to know who is sharing or not sharing, painting or spilling the paint, building or knocking over the blocks, drawing on paper or on the walls; and it requires a great deal of physical balance and agility to spin around at a moment's notice to prevent an accident from happening. Many aspects of early childhood curricula can be unabashedly challenging to the older teacher's sense of competence.

We can respond by asserting that early childhood education should be inclusive of its older and more experienced teachers. But can we modify our preschools to be truly inclusive of them? Sadly, very few studies have looked into this aspect of early childhood teaching—how older teachers in early years' education cope, what keeps them going, and whether or how the working environment can enable or frustrate their efforts. Based on my experience, older teachers—women, in particular—may require adjustments to their employment arrangements such as shorter working hours or job-sharing opportunities. In fact, to me, job-sharing between a younger and older teacher is a good way of harnessing the strengths of both worlds; the physical energy of the younger lady and the wisdom and experience of the other.

But we have to ask ourselves the hard question too. Would older teachers want to step aside themselves, acknowledging their changing physical, psychological, and perhaps even, social circumstances? Many women in midlife are caregivers to elderly parents and maybe even grandchildren, all while managing their own ageing.

More than 30 years ago, the educational scholar, Michael Huberman, undertook a large study in which he examined the life cycles of teachers.[146] He found that the development of a teacher's career is not unlike the sequence experienced by those in other professions. Specifically, a career is a **process** that may be linear or stage-like, and which may be marked by "regressions, dead-ends, and unpredictable changes of direction sparked by new realisations—in short, discontinuities".

For the older teacher, Huberman discovered that a discontinuity may happen at mid-career, somewhere between the 15th and 25th year of teaching. During this phase, the teacher may start to draw up a balance sheet of her professional life and contemplate—sometimes with anxiety—other careers during the short time that she has left when a career change is still possible. Huberman describes this as a kind of reassessment that for female teachers may start at around the age of 39 and continue to age 45. Importantly, the reassessment may be sparked by a desire for professional advancement, especially for male teachers, but for female teachers, it usually hinges on issues such as working conditions or job satisfaction.

A few years after her departure, I learnt that the older teacher who had left Wee Care on account of her menopause symptoms had moved to a neighbouring ASEAN nation. Interestingly, she had taken on the role of an educational leader/administrator in a preschool, different from what she had been doing previously as a class teacher.

Most would assume that this new role was a well-deserved promotion. But I think that this teacher's decision should also be understood in the light of her very understandable attempt to avoid tedium, to seek new stimulation, ideas, commitments, and challenges. As Patricia Sikes explains, "ageing, occupational development, and identity are inextricably linked". Different attitudes, perspectives, frustrations, and concerns are related to different phases of the teacher's life and career progression.[147]

Eventually, however, Huberman discovered that older teachers disengage from their job completely. This withdrawal may be preceded by a stage of serenity and relational distance in which they feel they have less to prove to themselves or to others; or because there is a generational gap, anyway, with their younger students. It may also be characterised by conservatism (e.g. rigidity, dogmatism, or resistance towards innovation) and/or complaints (e.g. about local educational policies being ineffective or perplexing; or younger colleagues being less serious or committed). The detachment happens gradually. There is, at the beginning, a growing indifference to professional commitments. This is followed by overt decisions to spend more time on one's self, on activities outside of one's work, as well as more discerning and thoughtful pursuits.

I had certainly entered a different season of feeling and being by early 2015. For one, I was questioning more and more my continued value in and for the company. I felt that I had already achieved everything that I had set out to do—establish a play-based preschool that was authentically inclusive in every respect. The early intervention outreach that we had established for children with special needs was also reputable, effective, and for some, life-changing. In addition, I had managed to resolve most of the issues related to HR recruitment and retention. This had constituted the "last frontier" for me because staffing problems had been, for so many years, solidly intractable in so many ways. What was left to conquer?

At the same time, I had learnt so much through the Doctor in Education (EdD) programme that there were other ways I could (or perhaps should) influence early childhood education in Singapore (and Asia) for the better. Poverty and socio-economic inequalities (from the time young children enter school) had come up as a significant reason, front and centre in my thesis, for the ongoing class divide in Singapore society. It did not take me long to reason that if I could teach or train younger teachers in a more concerted manner, these teachers would be able to, as a group, effect more change for the children of the future than myself alone.

Furthermore, I had witnessed that real and widespread change can look more like a game of dominoes, or that of widening ripples on the surface of water, than direct efforts to break new ground. Over time, perhaps on account of the pioneering work that we had achieved, positive changes had taken root—slowly but surely—in other early childhood education and early intervention settings in Singapore. Some preschools had copied our philosophy, practices, and policies, and they had perhaps sparked other copycats of their own. But the competitive marketplace had also forced many of these preschools to distinguish and improve the quality of their methods and systems of delivery so that by the 2010s, there were many other options for parents to choose from when selecting a kindergarten or therapy centre for their child.

In short, there was no need for me to pioneer anything more, no need to think that early childhood education or early intervention in Singapore was still an area of wilderness or barrenness; for surely it was not. It seemed that my time was coming to an end, and yet, there was no one who seemed interested in taking over the helm at Wee Care from me. My daughters were still in school, and both my husband and I had agreed that we would not burden any of them with a long-term obligation that they would not be able to make sense of till later, or worse, might not even want after they had understood the implications.

It has been said that "the unfolding of a career is, after all, a story of waxing or waning satisfaction, commitment, and competence".[148] I was most certainly on the wane, but what I did not expect at all was that an external reason would end up being the ultimate push factor for my time at Wee Care.

This cause (or rather, force) looked to me—at the time—like an encroaching army of invaders swarming the land, taking all prisoner with its laws, rules, and regulations. It seemed that the garden I had planted through back-breaking work was about to be harshly manicured and severely pruned; along with the other gardens that had sprouted next to it! The future, once full of promise and possibilities, began to look strange. Whenever I contemplated the way ahead, I saw a land filled with lots of pretty gardens everywhere but toiled in by soldiers, not landscapers. In short, what was on the horizon looked to me like the onset of a new and different (perhaps even difficult) early childhood sector where teachers would unwittingly have a reduced sense of professional autonomy and freedom, less fertile grounds to exercise their powers of creativity and innovation, and most of all, a sore lack of that very scarce and precious commodity, time.

I tried to push my anxieties away but could not. Trepidation became a constant companion.

144 Lin, S. L. (2019, August 24). Watch for casual ageism and other signs of caustic attitudes about older workers. *Channel NewsAsia*. https://www.channelnewsasia.com/news/commentary/casual-ageism-retirement-re-employment-cpf-raise-65-11835382
145 Ball, S. J., & Goodson, I (Eds.). (1985). *Teachers' lives and careers*. London, UK: Falmer Press. See also, Goodson, I., & Hargreaves, A. (Eds.). (1996). *Teachers' professional lives*. London, UK: Falmer Press.
146 Huberman, M. (1993). *The lives of teachers*. New York, NY: Teachers College Press.
147 Sikes, P. J. (1985). The life cycle of the teacher. In S. J. Ball & I. F. Goodson (Eds.), *Teachers' lives and careers* (pp. 27–60). London, UK: Falmer Press.
148 Huberman, M., Thompson, C. L., & Weiland, S. (1997). Perspectives on the teaching career. In B. J. Biddle, T. L. Good, & I. F. Goodson (Eds.), *International Handbook of Teachers and Teaching* (pp. 11–77). Dordrecht, the Netherlands: Springer.

13

WALKING AWAY

My first act of resistance (if you would call it that) against early childhood policy in Singapore revolved, quite unfortunately, around a matter of considerable personal significance: my qualifications. Around the time Wee Care initiated the process of registering as a kindergarten, I had already commenced studies towards my Doctor in Education (EdD) degree. The degree was similar to your typical PhD but designed for professionals in education and education-related fields. So, for all intents and purposes, the way I understood it at least, it was a "professional PhD".

The programme was just as rigorous as the traditional degree, if not more so, because I had embarked on a dual degree. There were expectations to meet at both my "home" university at the National Institute of Education Singapore (NIE) and later, at the Institute of Education in London (IoE). If my memory serves me right, I had to maintain a grade point average (GPA) of no less than a B for the compulsory modules if I wanted to progress to the "next stage"—an

Institution-Focused Study (IFS) (equivalent, I was told, to a Master's dissertation) **before** the final dissertation. Clearing all of these hoops was stressful, to say the least. It seemed like there was always one extra hoop to jump through. There were even supplementary "reflection" papers to write for the IFS and dissertation!

> I have been here before,
> this moment between 1:00 am and 5:00 am
> where the world stops still and all I hear is the breathing
> yours and mine
> circulating
> air patterns
> through the diapers of our dreams
> catching
> memories
> while the bright and morning star looks on.

Looking back, I have no idea how I managed to finish the degree. I can only credit God for the grace He gave me to endure, and for the love and encouragement I received from my husband, children, mother, and Wee Care staff, especially the managers who held the fort so capably and without complaint when I took an urgent six-week sabbatical to finish writing. During this last phase, when I was due to be examined in London, the IoE was also incredibly supportive, as was my dissertation supervisor, Professor Iram Siraj.

This journey of my **becoming** a teacher[149] was different to the usual route taken by most kindergarten teachers in Singapore. I had, for one, never considered doing the requisite diploma in kindergarten teaching endorsed by the Singapore Ministry of Education (MOE) because my professional and research interests upon graduating from NUS extended beyond the realm of preschool education only. I had a deep interest, for instance, in topics pertaining to special education in addition to neurotypical child development, language acquisition, early literacy, and play. I was to find, in the mid-1990s, that only a postgraduate degree—in this case, the Master's degree in Education from Sheffield University—allowed me the freedom and flexibility to delve into each of these areas. There were no rigid boundaries in this programme concerning the age group of children I was interested in studying; no barriers to crossing the early years, primary years, and even special education when accessing content or writing up papers. The dissertation I wrote for this degree was an exploratory study of borderline children in Singapore, that subgroup of students whose intellectual profiles fall in the space between "normal" and "challenged". These students struggle in mainstream schools in Singapore but outperform their schoolmates by a mile in special schools. Criss-crossing subject matter domains like this, I learnt a lot, knowledge-wise, but also the benefits of not allowing myself to be confined unnecessarily to strict man-made rules. To some, I may have looked like a generalist. But I accrued know-how and skills in certain **specialist** areas too; enough to feel confident about **owning** my practice as a teacher to both young children and young children with special needs.

Years later, I would discover, quite unfortunately, that this decision to sidestep the diploma would present something of a stumbling block to Wee Care. Specifically, when I tried to have myself recognised as Wee Care's kindergarten principal, I was told I did not have the necessary qualifications to be registered. I was qualified, but not qualified. I did not have the state-endorsed diploma to be cleared as a kindergarten principal. Furthermore, I was made to understand, at the time, that I could not leapfrog into doing the leadership diploma without first completing the basic diploma in preschool teaching. The entire policy felt regressive and outdated.

You can retain your rights as the owner of the preschool, can't you? Just employ a kindergarten principal.

Even now, the memory of conversations like this with the preschool unit of the Singapore MOE raises my hackles. It was even more infuriating when I learnt that the entire process of registering the kindergarten could be scuppered on just this one sticking point. In other words, a kindergarten could not exist without a principal, but that principal had to be an "employee". What happens then, I reasoned, when that principal resigns? Does the preschool cease operations during those months when there is no principal, which may well happen during staff transitions? Does it go back into operation when a new principal is hired? Were there no concessions for when the owner/operator was herself qualified? Ah, but herein was the rub again; to the MOE, I was not.

The inflexibility was to me, simply bewildering. But more crucially, knowing how serious the problem of staff turnover was in the early childhood sector in Singapore, I became all the more resolute about registering myself as Wee Care's principal, until a suitable principal could be found anyway. This way, Wee Care would be less vulnerable to shifts in staffing over time.

There was a great deal of back-and-forth with the MOE where it became apparent they would not concede or even budge a little. In the end, I was so frustrated I wrote to the Minister of Education. Within a day or so, I received an email from the same department I had been liaising with, asking if I would please come to the unit for a meeting.

It was a tense meeting, but to his credit, the Director I met was very tolerant and patient with me. He asked for a detailed breakdown of the subjects and topics I had studied over the years, and eventually came back with a proposal.

"Would you be willing," he asked, "to fulfil the one module you do not seem to have completed through your undergraduate and postgraduate studies, which is to undertake a supervised practicum with one of our training providers?"

I had already researched, prior to this proposal, the ways in which other countries like the United Kingdom, the United States, and Australia managed teacher registrations. Hence, I knew that this manner of becoming a registered teacher (called "licensing", "certification", or "accreditation" in other parts of the world) was not unique to Singapore only. What I resisted was the dogmatism that prevented the inclusion and accommodation of individuals who were just as able to work in the early childhood sector, or who had already demonstrated by their years of service that they had a heart for, and commitment to, young children and their families. I was also aghast that by imposing a ceiling on "acceptable" qualifications, competency levels in the sector would end up being artificially squashed. Dark thoughts of social stratification and its interplay with power and politics (a.k.a. Max Weber's theory) only served to make me more cross.[150]

Hence, when this olive branch was extended, I was pleasantly surprised and more than willing to cooperate. I dutifully reached out to the training providers at the time and Dr Lucy Quek (then Deputy Director of the School of Humanities and Social Sciences at Ngee Ann Polytechnic) took me on as an "adult student". I did not appreciate the extra work I had to do as part of the practicum (in addition to what I was already shouldering at Wee Care and for the EdD) but Lucy was very kind, patient, and encouraging. I was and still am very grateful to her. When the practicum was finally over and my registration as Wee Care's principal was finally approved, I was hugely relieved.

Since then, I have found out that this concessionary process of having one's qualifications vetted by the relevant authority—namely, ECDA (Early Childhood Development Authority)—and training gaps plugged in a modular way, is now the de facto procedure for individuals with different or overseas certificates.[151] While the process is still somewhat tiresome and stressful, it provides some measure of hope to individuals who have taken the road less travelled. Some teachers, for example, might be competent early childhood professionals who have trailed a spouse to Singapore. Around 2016, we managed (after another round of emails) to register an American teacher who had already obtained her licence to teach within the state of Texas in the United States.

ECDA's system of teacher certification is more comprehensive and inclusive now. It affords many "pathways" to **becoming** an early childhood educator in Singapore. In fact, the present model acknowledges that becoming a teacher is a process. More importantly, this flexibility must go some way in alleviating the shortfall of trained early years' professionals that we have in Singapore.

To me, however, the system as it stands today, will always be juxtaposed against the considerable exasperation I felt in the past. Indeed, the frustration I experienced at the time was quite remarkable. I am sure there were other teachers and centres who communicated similar feelings and feedback to the MOE/ECDA then.

Nothing though, could have prepared me for the tsunami of emotions, especially of shock and bewilderment, that swept through my world following the 2012 publication of *Starting Well* by the Economist Intelligence Unit.[152] This report—commissioned by the Lien Foundation, a Singapore-based philanthropic organisation—benchmarked early education around the world and ranked Singapore preschools a grim 29 out of the 45 nations studied (below South Korea at 10 and Hong Kong at 19). Some of the criteria that contributed to Singapore's poor standing included the evaluation that local classrooms had, on average, a student-teacher ratio above 15 to 1; teachers who were not particularly well-trained in early childhood education; and the lack of legislation guaranteeing children the legal right to a preschool education.

Let me quickly say here that it was not Singapore's placing per se that alarmed me. In fact, when the Index was released and the results publicised in all of the national broadsheets in Singapore, I gave a sigh of relief because here, at last, was some acknowledgement of the challenging conditions preschools were operating in, and please could we get some appreciation plus tangible forms of help and support? I felt optimistic even that things would improve, that the government would step in and play a more significant role in supporting teachers and owners/operators, plus fund preschool education for all children in Singapore.

I was wrong. Not only was there no appreciation extended nor tangible forms of funding given (that did not have extensive and laborious conditions attached to them), preschools were blamed.

In fact, preschool teachers were blamed.

Preschool administrators were blamed.

Preschool operators were blamed.

They were blamed for poor standards.
They were blamed for poor processes.
They were blamed for everything.

The only one who did not seem to be blamed was the Government itself. Okay, I would admit that perhaps my memories are clouded and I am exaggerating the extent of the criticism perceived. But I definitely sensed a different tone in all of my direct and indirect interactions with the authorities thereafter. It seemed to me that having been judged to be a problem, preschools and preschool teachers in the sector were now deemed to be in urgent need of fixing. While there were certainly issues that needed addressing, I found the experience of being ordered around and told what to do, by those who had never seemingly spent a day in a preschool classroom, somewhat unfair and unpleasant.

Let me rewind a little here to say that as fully argued in both *Starting Well* and *Vital Voices for Vital Years*[153] as well as in my own doctoral research, state funding of preschool education for young children is necessary because huge resources are required to "provide for high-quality early childhood education, free of charge and accessible to all". [154]

Left to market forces, and as explained earlier, preschools stratify on the basis of how much parents can pay, and this, in turn, affects the young child's access to good-quality schooling. Over time, socio-economic disparities perpetuate through the early childhood system. In the case of Singapore, this can happen as early as the infant or toddler years, when parents select childcare centres for their babies and/or when toddlers have their first forays into playgroup or pre-nursery programmes. As one respondent remarked in *Vital Voices for Vital Years*: "You can pay $100 to $1,000 to put a child in preschool education and each preschool offers you something different".[155]

Examining the countries in a comparative manner, the *Starting Well* Index showed that Nordic countries perform the best at preschool. In fact, the preschool systems of European countries dominated the top 20 spots on the Index. This showing par excellence was credited to "sustained, long-term investments and prioritisation of early childhood development". Not only are there comprehensive strategies in these nations to promote early childhood development, preschool attendance in most of these countries has also been instituted as a legal right. As a result, preschool provision has gradually become a universal norm. Even when provisions are privatised, the cost to enrol in such care or education is affordable, relative to average wages in the country.

Some want to call this kind of a preschool system, "nationalised". To me, you can call it anything you want. A rose by any other name would smell as sweet.

But far was the scenario of glorious redemption that I had envisaged for early childhood education in Singapore, the kind that would liberate us all from the shackles of stress and unhappiness that had pervaded our experiences as teachers and owners/operators. In fact, the months and years following 2012 felt like a nightmare at times. We (owners/operators and preschool professionals) were invited at different times for focus group discussions and larger meetings to share our views, opinions, and experiences on all sorts of matters. Reflecting on each of these meetings afterwards, I was more inclined to conclude that ECDA's[156] main goal was to **tell** us something instead:

... that we had to be more careful with the children—"A teacher scalded a child by accident, tsk tsk ..."

... that minimum requirements on teacher qualifications would be raised—"Teachers will need a minimum B4 at the GCE "O" Level English Language paper please ..."

... that it was important to improve standards—"SPARK (the Singapore Preschool Accreditation Framework) is your companion for your centre's quality improvement journey ..."

And many, many more regulatory requirements, sometimes to the minutest detail, as time passed. Not just the usual specifications for fire safety, toilet seats, and sinks plus important health and hygiene measures, mind you, but eventually too, ultimatums for extra rooms/space and even, smells! Yes, smells; or non-smells (ventilation) to be precise, as was the problem sometimes, we were told, for kindergartens or childcare centres located in the void decks of HDB blocks and sited too close to refuse collection points.

Not that any of these requirements are wrong in themselves as obviously, young children deserve the very best forms of care and education. Neither was I worried about Wee Care's standards for health and safety, teacher professionalism, or teaching quality. Oh, no. Our drive for excellence over the years meant that I was confident Wee Care had all of the necessary statutory approvals to operate, plus very good protocols in place for all of our students, families, and teachers alike. In fact, reading the prerequisites that an Early Childhood Development Centre (ECDC) must meet for registration approval[157] these days, I cannot help but feel inwardly pleased that some of the stated requirements—such as a Parent Handbook and Standard Operating Procedures (or SOPs) for child guidance and behaviour management—were instituted at Wee Care more than a decade ago!

No, for me, the point of contention at the time was that demands were being made on owners/operators and teachers without any assurance of financial support for the increased costs that would invariably result from these demands. Take the case of early childhood centres at the void decks, for example, many of which are run by non-profit organisations. When I first heard that "smells" would be one of the criteria for "standards", I pondered at the solutions available for these centres. Would air-conditioning work to remove all undesirable smells? If yes, who would be paying for their installation, maintenance, and ongoing electricity costs? Would government grants[158] be able to cover the increase? If no, would the centre have to move? HDB would not be able to re-site a refuse collection point, not when it is already part of the main structure of a block of flats. If the early childhood centre was forced to move, who would be paying the costs of the relocation; specifically, renovation of the new site and reinstatement of the old one? Also, what about other non-profit schools that do not have access to government grants (as in the case of church kindergartens)? The more I thought about it, the more astounded I became at what ECDA was doing **to** the sector, not just **for** the sector.

I say this because overshadowing the "standards" framework that ECDA was slowly initiating all of us into were simultaneous policy initiatives to reshape and consolidate the preschool market in Singapore into something of an oligopoly. These initiatives included the expansion of the Anchor Operator Scheme (AOP)[159] and the creation, in 2016, of the Partner Operator Scheme (POP).[160] In both programmes, centres are required to keep their fees low in exchange for government funding and priority in securing new sites. In 2017, it was estimated that between 2012 to 2020, the market share held by these anchor and partner operators would grow to about 50%.[161]

In addition to these preferred players, the government also threw the sector another curveball: the introduction, in 2014, of MOE Kindergartens. Located mostly within local primary schools, MOE Kindergartens are the closest the Singapore government has come to nationalising preschool education. Fees are low[162] and places are allocated in priority order, for example, if the child is a Singapore citizen from a household with a gross household income not exceeding $3,500 a month or a per capita income not exceeding $875 a month, and who lives within 1 km of the kindergarten.[163]

The demand for MOE Kindergartens has grown year-on-year,[164] spurred, many believe, by another benefit. To "help children transition more smoothly to Primary 1, those attending Ministry of Education (MOE) kindergartens will be given priority to enter the primary school that shares a compound with their kindergarten".[165] In the ultra-competitive process that tends to characterise Primary 1 admissions in Singapore, this is nothing short of a ticket to substantial peace-of-mind for the concerned parent, especially one who lives in a neighbourhood filled with many other young families.

Viewed from the outset and from the outside, MOE Kindergartens are a really good thing. They meet a real need for good-quality preschool education at an affordable price. Moreover, children's access to these schools will increase as more and more MOE Kindergartens are added over time.[166]

Set within the current "free market", however, MOE Kindergartens are an extra source of competition for private (and these include non-profit) providers who are already grappling with space/land constraints, high rents, staff shortages, and now, the pressure to keep fees low. They also send a clear signal of delineation to all early childhood centres, something of a "me-versus-you" mentality.

If we have to nationalise preschool education in Singapore, we will do it our way, without any reliance on or collaboration with you.

All of my hopes that private preschools like Wee Care would be absorbed into a national system of preschool education—much like how primary and secondary schools started by clan associations, philanthropists, and community or religious groups in the past were slowly converted into national schools by a grant-giving scheme[167]— were totally and completely dashed with this development. It was a shock to me too (although, perhaps, it should not have been) that the government would begin the process of "nationalisation"—regardless of whether they wished to call it, or admit to, this or not—in this economically- and politically-expedient manner. For by assuming the roles of both regulator and player in the free market of preschool education, the government succeeded in retaining enormous control while simultaneously buying itself public goodwill ("we are doing something") and valuable time in the process. Organised this way, it could recalibrate its budget and increase its technical capabilities and preschool teaching workforce gradually without having yet to shoulder full (financial and operational) responsibility for the sector.

In my view, however, they did this at the immense cost of alienating many early childhood professionals and preschools that had, for countless years, educated Singapore's young. No, let me be more precise. They did this at the cost of small- and medium-sized kindergartens "bleeding" to death. In addition to long-standing constraints in funding and human resources, these preschools (including Wee Care) would now have to face the added stress of extra competition from both the government and government-supported big brands.

You should not be surprised, so said a wise man once to me.

Notwithstanding, as the owner of a private preschool, this turn of events was difficult. It begged the question of what I should do, knowing that the writing was on the wall.

Should I close Wee Care down, the company that I had built up for so many years from absolutely nothing, or should I take a wait-and-see approach?

Eventually, it was the introduction of the government's most formidable weapon that drove me to a decision. When the Early Childhood Development Centres Act (or ECDC Act) was first suggested in 2015, I recoiled at the way the Bill had been drafted and the severity of the penalties proposed. The draft was shockingly punitive. For instance, at one very large "sector briefing", we were told that preschool principals would be fined $10,000 and face a jail term of 12 months if they recruited a teacher without the necessary government-approved qualifications. Coming on the heels of my very own negative experiences concerning "qualifications", I was furious. There was still a very serious shortage of trained and experienced teachers available in Singapore—was ECDA keen on sending us some of their best officers to help out in our classrooms while we sourced for these "approved" teachers?

There were other heavy-handed measures too; including ones that gave the government the right to "enter and search", and to determine:

... the admission of children by their age into the right "class or type of centre";

... the kind of curriculum or programme the centre was permitted to carry out; and

"... the fees and other charges to be paid in respect of the services provided in the centres or otherwise ... and the restriction or prohibition of any further fees and charges".

Most of all, there was the shocking waiver of MOE Kindergartens from the same statutes.

It felt completely surreal and yet, it was real. So real, and so threatening.

I could not, for one, reconcile the math of paying high rents and good salaries out of a smaller revenue base of potentially restricted fees from Wee Care's smaller enrolment. For surely, based on the policy changes, something would have to give: Either I would have to pay my teachers less, or increase the teacher-student ratio in each classroom significantly. But never a mega childcare centre for me![168] One of Wee Care's most enduring commitment, from the time of its inception, was to smaller class sizes and individualised care. It was unthinkable, in my mind, to go back on my word to families and children who needed this, especially the students with special learning needs.

I could not, at the same time, accept the forced cessation of all of my creative convictions and professional freedoms. For with the Act, I would become nothing more than a bureaucrat myself, a local administrator of rules and records, a micromanager of teachers' actions and decisions, day-in and day-out. If I chose to delegate the task of record-keeping and reporting to an administrator, it would be an additional headcount or even two (and thus more costs for the school) in addition to the staff I already had.

But most of all, I could not stomach the manner in which the government was shouting its distrust of everyone and every school in the sector, without acknowledging all of the good that had been done, all of the sacrifices and dedication that had been ploughed into the land, all of the life that had been sown and reaped. Some might call me reactive and hypersensitive, for where or what was there anything **personal** in what the government was trying to do?

It's not about you, Denise, and it's not about Wee Care.

But it was, and still is, about people. Teaching is about teachers and children and families and relationships, and policies can cultivate or destroy these, if done without compassion, empathy, and respect. Just consider the implications:

... of teachers feeling so exhausted by the increased demands exacted by the Act that fewer join the sector and many leave;

... of smaller and/or niche preschools closing down because the financial figures make absolutely no sense anymore;

... of a workforce that focuses on ticking the boxes rather than on tickling children's imaginations;

... of children with special needs facing reduced options when trying to access good-quality intervention and education in small, secure, and inclusive environments.

This last scenario would have been my biggest heartbreak—knowing that the inclusivity we had worked so hard to achieve over the years could and would so easily be uprooted by the changes that were being sought and wrought by ECDA. The more I thought about the Bill and its repercussions, the sadder I became.

The ECDC Bill (modified after a public consultation)[169] was eventually ratified in Parliament on the 28 February 2017. You can read the Act for yourself[170] and decide whether it is fair and necessary, or simply another case of Singapore authoritarianism expressing itself through law.[171] Or perhaps, I should be kinder and fairer myself: Does the Act regulate or over-regulate? Will it achieve its goal of higher standards? If yes, what manner of higher standards and at what costs?

Like salt in a wound, I was also painfully aware that while a law had been passed controlling teachers and providers, no law had been passed to improve the student-teacher ratio or to guarantee children in Singapore the right to a preschool education.

So, in a way, what else is there to discuss, my friend? I can only mourn.

There were good questions in Parliament pertaining to the Bill,[172] most of which were ignored by the local dailies. I knew about the reading only because Leon Perera, a friend of mine and Member of

Parliament for Aljunied GRC (Group Representation Constituency), had alerted me to it. To be honest, I find it hard to process the government's responses to the questions. They are filled with puzzling assertions, such as:

> "There are very good small players ... but unfortunately, probably not able to scale up because a lot of its success is centred around the person who is driving the programme. It is very manpower intensive, which may be difficult to scale";

> "We did not want to drive it down from the top; many different stakeholders have been consulted. Where there were areas of concern, we have gone back and forth for a slightly longer period of time to take on board their feedback";

> "Many of the smaller centres appreciate the fact that some of these guidelines and some of these parameters are set, as these allow them to bring themselves up to a higher standard, because they do not have the scale or the resources necessarily to level themselves up on their own";

> "We have been in constant dialogue. Our whole effort is not about penalising and weeding out the smaller players. It is actually about helping those in the industry who are passionate about educating our children. How do we help them to level up? It is very

much, as I have mentioned earlier, a developmental approach that we are taking";

"We are working very closely with many of the special needs centres, and many of them do not have a huge concern in transiting to this new regime";

"... we do not require operators to employ designated administrative or compliance staff. Most operators should be able to manage the new framework with their existing resources";

"We do not anticipate there to be significant cost increases as a result of this Act. Why do we say this? In the process of coming up with this Act, we have been working very closely with the industry on how to unfold this, how these various measures would kick-in in very practical terms."[173]

To this day, it is a mystery to me how each of these statements could so conclusively express a view of reality so unlike my own, so dissimilar to life on the ground for Wee Care and the teachers/preschools I was in touch with. But this is Singapore after all, so the Bill passed without difficulty. From my later analysis, most of the regulations encapsulated in the Act were calibrated upwards of the 2015 draft, to an even more meticulous and prescriptive degree, resulting in a most burdensome set of directives.

We will not be unreasonable.
But a different administration might.

Yet I also knew that there was no point engaging in an extended petition[174] or sending repeated emails to the authorities. Many Singaporeans trust the government unequivocally, and there are good reasons for this trust. Nonetheless, as Cherian George puts it so eloquently in his classic volume, *Singapore: The Air-Conditioned Nation*, comfort is achieved through control."[175]

Indeed.

For myself though, I could not imagine operating Wee Care in an environment that was both legalistic and restrictive. I did not want to be a cog in the wheel of a large machine, turning and turning to comply rather than to create and inspire. Thus, for quite a while after the Bill was passed, I firmly believed that it would be better for Wee Care to close rather than to change its fundamental values. It would be less of a struggle for the school as an entity too, because there was no way we could maintain the quality of care and education we were known for in the face of these additional pressures and costs.

I must have been quite sad, because one day, out of the blue, I received an email from a friend of mine (a former Wee Care mother).

I had a dream last night. It was the annual storytelling event. But it was so different. It felt so sad. Is something wrong? Can I help?

A competent businesswoman, she met with me almost immediately and talked me through the options. With her advice, and the ongoing support and advice of my husband, my co-director Andrew, and other business experts, Wee Care was put on the market quietly. We had four interested buyers within a few weeks. I settled on one of them, the one whom I felt had the most sincere commitment to children with special needs as well as the business acumen to ride out what I anticipated would be a very rough season ahead. The sale was completed by the end of 2017 and I handed over the leadership and management reins of the company by the end of May 2018.

In this way, I was able to retain the life of the school as well as the employment of many individuals and the education of many children. It was not easy walking away, but it was far easier than bringing the life I had borne to a close.

---

149 Kohl, H. R. (1986). *On becoming a teacher*. London, UK: Methuen.
150 Weber, M. (2006). Class, status, party. In R. F. Levine (Ed.), *Social class and stratification: Classic statements and theoretical debates* (2nd ed., pp. 49–62). Lanham, MD: Rowman & Littlefield Publishers.
151 For more information, see Early Childhood Development Agency. (2020, December). *Teacher Certification Application (for Applicants with Foreign Early Childhood Qualifications)*.
https://www.ecda.gov.sg/Educators/Pages/For-those-with-foreign-Early-Childhood-qualifications.aspx
152 The EIU is the research and analysis division of The Economist Group, the sister company to *The Economist* newspaper. The *Starting Well* report may be found at:
https://www.lienfoundation.org/uploads/Early%20Childhood%20Development/Starting%20Well%20Index/StartingWell_Index_Report_Full%20[pdf].pdf
153 Ang, L. (2012). *Vital voices for vital years: A study of leaders' perspectives on improving the early childhood sector in Singapore*. Singapore: Lien Foundation.
154 World Congress of Education International (1998). *Resolution on early childhood education*. https://www.ei-ie.org/en/detail/14583/resolution-on-early-childhood-education
155 From page 38 of Ang, L. (2012). *Vital voices for vital years: A study of leaders' perspectives on improving the early childhood sector in Singapore*. Singapore: Lien Foundation.
156 The Early Childhood Development Authority (ECDA) was established on 1 April 2013, soon after the publication of the *Starting Well* report.
157 Early Childhood Development Authority (2020). *Guide to setting up an Early Childhood Development Centre* (ECDC). Singapore: ECDA.
https://www.ecda.gov.sg/Documents/Resources/Guide%20to%20Setting%20up%20ECDC.pdf
158 For more information, please see: Ministry of Social and Family Development. (2020, March 5). *Enhanced Support For Preschool Operators And Families*. https://www.msf.gov.sg/media-room/Pages/Enhanced-Support-for-Preschool-Operators-and-Families.aspx
159 For more information about the AOP scheme, please see: Early Childhood Development Agency. (n.d.). *ECDA Anchor Operator Scheme (AOP)*. https://www.ecda.gov.sg/Parents/Pages/AOP.aspx

160 For more information about the POP scheme, please see: Early Childhood Development Agency. (n.d.). *ECDA Partner Operator Scheme (POP)*. https://www.ecda.gov.sg/Parents/Pages/POP.aspx

161 Goy, P. (2017, March 19). What the new playing field for preschool offers. *The Straits Times*. https://www.straitstimes.com/singapore/what-the-new-playing-field-for-pre-school-offers

162 Current fees may be found here: Ministry of Education, Singapore. (n.d.). *MOE Kindergarten fees*. https://moe.gov.sg/preschool/moe-kindergarten/fees/

163 For more information, see: Ministry of Education, Singapore. (n.d.). *Register for MOE Kindergarten: Priority admission and balloting*. https://moe.gov.sg/preschool/moe-kindergarten/register/priority-admission/

164 Syed, N. (2018, March 20). MOE Kindergartens increasing in demand. *The Educator Online*. https://www.theeducatoronline.com/he/archived/moe-kindergartens-increasing-in-demand/247893

165 For more information, please see Davie, S. (2017, November 28). MOE Kindergarten pupils to get priority in P1 entry. *The Straits Times*. https://www.straitstimes.com/singapore/education/moe-kindergarten-pupils-to-get-priority-in-p1-entry

166 Sixty kindergartens will be opened by 2025: Ministry of Education, Singapore. (n.d.). *Overview of MOE Kindergarten*. https://moe.gov.sg/preschool/moe-kindergarten/overview/

167 Lim, L. C. (2007). Many pathways, one mission: Fifty years of Singapore education. Singapore: Curriculum Planning & Development Division, Ministry of Education.

168 For more information about mega childcare centres, please see: Early Childhood Development Agency. (2017, January 18). Four more large child care centres to open by 2018. https://www.ecda.gov.sg/pressreleases/pages/four-more-large-child-care-centres-to-open-by-2018.aspx

169 Early Childhood Development Agency (2015). *Public consultation on proposed Early Childhood Development Centres Regulatory Framework: Summary of key feedback and responses*. REACH (Reaching Everyone for Active Citizenry @ Home). https://www.reach.gov.sg/participate/public-consultation/early-childhood-development-agency/public-consultation-on-proposed-early-childhood-development-centres-regulatory-framework

170 The Early Childhood Development Centres Act 2017 and its related regulations are available at: Early Childhood Development Centres Regulations 2018. No. S 890. https://sso.agc.gov.sg/SL-Supp/S890-2018/Published/20181228?DocDate=20181228 and at: Early Childhood Development Centres (Amendment) Regulations 2019. No. S 86. https://sso.agc.gov.sg/SL-Supp/S86-2019/Published/20190214?DocDate=20190214

171 Rajah, J. (2012). *Authoritarian rule of law: Legislation, discourse and legitimacy in Singapore*. New York, NY: Cambridge University Press.

172 To read the parliamentary debates around the Bill, please see: Parliament Singapore. (2017, February 28). *Official Reports, Parliamentary Debates: Early Childhood Development Centres Bill*. https://sprs.parl.gov.sg/search/email/link/?id=017_20170228_S0003_T00038fullContentFlag=false

173 Parliament Singapore. (2017, February 28). *Official Reports, Parliamentary Debates: Early Childhood Development Centres Bill*. https://sprs.parl.gov.sg/search/email/link/?id=017_20170228_S0003_T00038fullContentFlag=false

174 Opposition by preschools was reported in the press: Goy, P. (2015, August 17). Pre-schools oppose fines for admin lapses. *The Straits Times*. https://www.straitstimes.com/singapore/education/pre-schools-oppose-fines-for-admin-lapses

175 From page 18 of George, C. (2000). *Singapore, the air-conditioned nation: Essays on the politics of comfort and control*. Singapore: Landmark Books.

EPILOGUE

As I sit here at my desk writing, more than three years after selling Wee Care, I cannot help but reflect on life; not just the life that is defined as mine, but

>life in all of its
>goodness and badness,
>happiness and sadness,
>
>life with all of its
>ins-and-outs,
>ups-and-downs,
>ebbs and flows—
>
>the kind of life we seek, and the kind we choose not to,
>life when it is full, and life when it is empty—
>Life when it is no longer there.

Motherhood—the mother as one who gives life—has continued to grant me much life. By the time this book is published, my eldest daughter—the one whose quiet, solitary life as an infant prompted me to start Wee Care in the first place—will be married. The thought of new life through hers, that continuation we call a cycle, stirs feelings of gratitude, awe, and joy. Indeed, to see each of my daughters growing in their respective lots, flowering and fruiting in different ways and according to the seasons of **their lives**, is extraordinarily beautiful. I know that they will chart their own courses, develop their own views, and exercise their own ideals and ambitions.

In contrast, my womanhood, that global concept—the precise definition of which we, women, still grapple with over and over again—is slowly revealing its old and fading colours to no one more obviously than myself. The innate drive that took me from the maternity ward to work, from breastfeeding to another meeting, has been replaced by an acceptance of frailties and vagaries, a deep mellowness that I would not have understood in my younger and stronger but perhaps more insecure days. I am surprised that I am enjoying this new—and quieter—life. It is filled with conversations over meals, connections with those I love, and the company of close friends ... and those whom I can now call friends, for in the not-so-distant past, they were staff or clients and associates.

Interestingly, in this season of inevitable fading, life has continued to enrich and fill me, through reading and research, planning and teaching, writing and speaking. I am a different teacher to the one I was at Wee Care. The focus of my efforts and the students whom I respond to are different, but my work on behalf of young children and children with special needs continues in Singapore and beyond.

Life at Wee Care has gone on too, though not without considerable challenges. My heart goes out to the new management and staff, some of whom worked with me and are valuable assets, brave and kind and persistent. They hold the institutional memory of what the school was and to my delight, still is in many ways. Their new employers should be lauded for the ways in which they have sustained the school in the midst of ECDA's new and stringent guidelines, a forced move to new premises and a global pandemic. From what I have learnt, Wee Care has now also ventured into student care, an unexpected but not unpleasant surprise. More importantly, the work in early intervention has endured, under the supervision of a competent, hard-working, and experienced clinician whom I had the privilege of hiring and working with when I was in charge.

To my knowledge too, the Wee Care parents and children who were "mine" have also moved on. One tends to forget how fast children grow. Three years on and many are in primary school. The youngest then would be the oldest preschoolers now, and they would, in all likelihood, not remember me or know who I am. But it does not matter. I remember them, their faces especially, if not their names.

I remember many of their parents too and am delighted whenever I receive a call or text message from any one of them. I think—well, I hope anyway—that all of them have forgiven me for leaving. When news of the sale and my impending departure was announced, it was met with shock, horror, and disbelief. Some mothers cried, others came to my office filled with anxiety. Some asked very tough questions of the new management. I felt terrible for putting everyone through the anguish. But I hope that they understand, now, why it was necessary for me to go. No one is indispensable; in fact, in some cases (like mine), they should be dispensed of in order to achieve a greater good! Life then can go on without the baggage of an individual's particular temperament or unrealistic ideals.

But what of Singapore preschools and its teachers? What of the early childhood sector in our beloved country?

As I expected and warned, many local preschools (especially faith-based, not-for-profit kindergartens) have closed or are in danger of closing.[176] This trend—one that I anticipated in a 2015 blog post as a gradual and inexorable death—has prompted petitions and marketing campaigns from parents who are dismayed by the lack of choice they are facing. These parents want preschools where the principals and teachers know every child by name. They desire a learning environment where the child will be taught values; where his/her character and emotional skills can be nurtured and developed.

To give you a sense of the attrition, reports indicate that between 2012 and 2019, the number of faith-based preschools dropped by 50%, and "the numbers are still falling today".[177] The regret associated with their demise must be deep as some of these schools have a long history stretching back 60 years.[178] While some commentators have expressed concerns about the children and families affected by these closures, I think it is only to be expected that these students will simply be absorbed into one of the current "big boy" operators, thus increasing the latter's market share further.

Ironically, one of the emerging "big boys" is a faith-based consortium. In 2018, it was reported that St James' Church Kindergarten would step in to help "operate seven other faith-based preschools in a bid to keep them running and improve the quality of early childhood education".[179] These seven schools would be rebranded as Little Seeds Preschools and become a part of the St James' Preschool Services, a new arm of the church operator.

Interestingly, outside of the Anglican church that St James' Church Kindergarten is overseen by, four other church denominations (the Lutheran, Presbyterian, Bible-Presbyterian, and Methodist churches) banded together in 2019 to form the Christian Preschool Alliance, an interdenominational movement supporting Christian preschools in upholding specific values, standards, and goals. The Alliance subsequently set up a parallel non-profit organisation, Kingdomgarten Preschool Services, to provide "leadership, best practices, training, and support" to Christian preschools.[180] Their fear—but also their courage—is palpable. A thin banner at the top of their website describes the Christian preschool mission as "near collapsing".

As a Christian, I am happy that efforts are being made to keep these kindergartens alive. As a thinker, researcher, observer, and recent-insider, however, I worry about how successful these initiatives will be in the light of the play of power and politics in Singapore.

But even with these doubts, I am grateful.

There is evidence of life, after all.

And by this, I mean life as defined by acts of the human will, both personal and collective. For the energy that propels and constitutes life, that enacts itself in a determination to create and by its very nature, resist death, is a poignant reminder to me of the reasons that drove me into the wilderness so many years ago. It is an energy that should be celebrated, not shut down, although the shapes that it takes will continually change as more knowledge becomes available to us over time of children's needs, children's rights, and children's futures. It is an energy that emanates from and through people: teachers with dreams and passions, parents with hopes and aspirations, educational thinkers and leaders with vision, ideals, and ideas. It is dynamic, this life, an asset and

something that
should not be lost;
for I have been that teacher
parent
thinker
leader
and so have you
and so will you.

This threat of loss is real. Speaking with early childhood teachers in Singapore now, I hear anecdotes of:

... time spent "doing paperwork";
... hours covering an extra class or activity because there are insufficient teachers still;
... rigid requirements that reinforce a robotic compliance to rules rather than practical, creative, even common-sense solutions.*

And yet, we know that sustaining teachers' professional growth requires "manageable working conditions, opportunities—and

---

* In one funny but sad story recounted to me recently, a staff member at a preschool was asked about the school's cleaning procedures and cleaning logs. When she said that the teachers were well aware of their responsibilities, she was asked who was "enforcing" these duties and whether the school had a pest management system. When she asked if this meant the necessity of contracting an external service provider (which would constitute, mind you, an additional expense), she was asked how the school managed ants. When she replied matter-of-factly that she or any teacher would follow the trail of ants and remove the source that had caused the infestation, she was told that this was not enough, that the school needed a pest management system because it had pests!

sometimes demands—to experiment modestly without sanctions if things go awry". Teachers, over the years, have consistently reported that when they experience sustained support, they are able to cope and positively manage adverse circumstances. In other words, they are able to persevere in their jobs with resilience.[181]

We are doing the children of our nation a severe injustice when our teachers cannot be teachers. We are disrespecting them when we impose additional, perhaps even unnecessary, job functions that are different to their intended and desired calling. Most of all, we are disempowering them when we communicate, by the imposition of tough laws and policies, that they cannot think or judge effectively to make the right decisions for themselves and their students.

It has been said that "those of us who are teachers cannot stand before a class without standing for something ... teaching is testimony".[182] Indeed, we testify to what we love and what we value. We testify to whom we love and whom we value. But most of all, we—or perhaps, for now, it is still just I—testify to the knowledge that there is a better way for the early childhood sector in Singapore.

We can, surely ...

    cultivate without
    thorns or barbed wire
    heavy machines
    stripping
    shearing
    organising
    production into stern lines and plots;

so that we need not wonder why
our children cannot
think outside of the box

In this imagined, shared, collaborative, and inclusive space, I believe we can continue to bring forth life for everyone in the field and, with it, many more lifetimes of hope and positive outcomes for all of the children in our country.

"... He will make her wilderness like Eden,
and her desert like the garden of the Lord.
Joy and gladness shall be found therein,
thanksgiving and the voice of melody."[183]

---

176 Wong, P. T. (2019, July 16). Parents fight to keep non-profit preschools alive, as popularity of MOE kindergartens grows. *Today Online*. https://www.todayonline.com/singapore/parents-fight-keep-non-profit-preschools-alive-popularity-moe-kindergartens-grows

177 Tan, H. Y. (2019, August 2). Three denominations uniting to save Christian preschool education in Singapore. *Salt & Light*. https://saltandlight.sg/news/four-denominations-uniting-to-save-christian-preschool-education-in-singapore/

178 Teng, A. (2019, July 24). End of the road for small preschools in churches? *The Straits Times*. https://www.straitstimes.com/singapore/education/end-of-the-road-for-small-pre-schools-in-churches

179 Teng, A. (2018, December 3). 7 pre-schools to go under St James' Church Kindergarten umbrella. *The Straits Times*. https://www.straitstimes.com/singapore/education/7-pre-schools-to-go-under-st-james-church-kindergarten-umbrella

180 For more information, please see: Kingdomgarten Preschool Services. (n.d.). *Supporting Christian preschools in Singapore*. https://www.kingdomgarten.org/ and Kingdomgarten Preschool Services. (n.d.). About us. https://www.kingdomgarten.org/about-us

181 Day, C. (2012). New lives of teachers. *Teacher Education Quarterly, 39*(1), 7–26.

182 Paterson, L. J. (1991). *An evaluation of the Scottish pilot projects in the technical and vocational education initiative*. Edinburgh: Centre for Educational Sociology.

183 Isaiah 51:3. *The Holy Bible* (21st Century King James version).

ABOUT THE AUTHOR

Dr Denise Lai Chua was, between 1997 and 2018, the founder and Managing Director of the Wee Care Group Singapore, a company that provided both early childhood and early intervention programmes, including preschool inclusion, for children with additional learning needs. An experienced and highly-skilled early childhood practitioner and leader, Denise now spends her time writing, consulting, and training parents, early childhood educators, and special needs' educators around Asia through the Centre for Applied Practice in Education (CAPE) in Hong Kong. She is a Doctor in Education, an International Behaviour Analyst (IBA)™, and a Birkman Certified Professional (BCP). Her areas of research interest include social justice, power and politics in education, child and language development, Applied Behaviour Analysis, and a Theory of Mind. She blogs at www.makingripples.co.uk.

www.ingramcontent.com/pod-product-compliance
Lightning Source LLC
LaVergne TN
LVHW041805060526
838201LV00046B/1139